A GEOGRAPHER'S LOOK

at the

ISLE OF WIGHT

as told by

Roy Hollis

Comdr. R.N. (Ret'd.) F.C.P., F.R.G.S., Cert. Ed.

PUBLISHED BY CROSS PUBLISHING
NEWPORT, ISLE OF WIGHT

The Author

One time:-
Sailor, Teacher, Explorer, Industrialist, Writer, Lecturer, Councillor,
Consultant and, although a World Traveller, yet, still - only a
geography student!

First published in 1995
© Roy Hollis

British Library Cataloguing in Publication Data
A catalogue record for this book is available from the British Library

ISBN 1 873295 06 5

Published and designed by Cross Publishing, Newport, Isle of Wight
Printed by Crossprint, I.W.

Acknowledgements

I am grateful for the material help and suggestions given by Paul Airey, I.W. Council and by his assistant Rachel Jolliffe; also to David James, farmer and Alan Phillips, environmentalist who have kindly contributed ideas which are incorporated in Appendix IV.

Alan Doe, Second Master and Head of Geography, Bembridge School, I.W., an old friend and colleague has been good enough to check the script, although the opinions expressed and any mistakes are the author's.

To the many others from all over the Island from whom I have sought answers to my interminable questions - thank you for your patience.

All the sketches and most of the diagrams are derived from my original field work; the map outlines are based on aero-film, taken in 1963 and kindly given to me at that time, for another geographical study on "Brading Haven" (as yet unpublished), with the exception that the Land Use sketch map (Fig 43), interestingly, is from a loan photo taken from a satellite.

Author's Preface

Regrettably and probably because of the cost, there is no modern scholarship published as a book, on the "GEOGRAPHY OF THE ISLE OF WIGHT" even though on the micro scale, this Island abounds with serious academic study for the expert.

Yet, the story needs to be told and thus what follows, although written in a more simple form to avoid unnecessary technical jargon, is aimed, both, towards the median levels of "Geography in the National Curriculum" and, particularly, for the general interest of visiting schools and the many holidaymakers to help illuminate their stay on the I.W. It is, of course, a 'natural' for the bookshelf in every Island home.

Correct terminology has been used and key geographical terms in the text have been *italicized* (and are later explained in the **GLOSSARY** at the back of the book).

Regarding the format:-

1. *History is "chaps" whereas "Geography" is "maps"!* - being a convenient illustration to explain the absence of long-winded narrative when visual data will equally suffice.

2. *"All this beauty is of God"* - is the motto of the I.W. and was possibly behind the thinking of the young girl who attempted to explain the two main divisions in this book when she said - "Ah -

     (a) Physical Geography is what God made

and   (b) Human Geography is what people have done with it!"

3. *"I.W"* - as any true Islander knows, is the correct abbreviation for the "Isle of Wight" (i.e **not** "I.O.W.") and is used throughout.

4. *Reference Maps* - refer to O.S. Landranger 196 (Solent and the Isle of Wight) and to Institute of Geological Sciences - Special Sheet ("Isle of Wight") both in the 1:50,000 series.

5. *Sketch Maps and Diagrams* - apart from Fig 1, which has been drawn accurately, scale and direction have been deliberately omitted from all other sketch maps and diagrams - which have been drawn freehand and in most cases taken directly from the author's field notebooks.

6. *Census* - the last one in the twentieth century!
Except in 1941, a national Census has been taken every ten years since 1801. Unless otherwise stated all the statistical data in this book is based on the last Census, held in 1991.

7. *Extract* from the National Curriculum (November 1994)
"Pupils should be given opportunities to:-
(a) investigate the physical and human features of all the surroundings in their local areas
and
(b) undertake local studies that focus on geographical questions (e.g. "What/Where is it? What is it like? How does it fit in with the community?" etc.).

8. *Modern Geography* is a vast subject and, as is reflected in this book, nowadays it bridges both the Arts and Sciences in some depth. It is a dynamic study and, even in our smallest County in the Country, we can daily witness constant change in both its Physical and Human branches.

It is to be hoped that not too many changes will have occurred before you share this Geographer's Look at the Isle of Wight.

Contents

Contents

Contents

NARRATIVE

Contents

Contents

NARRATIVE

Page	*Section*	*Subject*

PART FOUR
Human Geography

Contents

──────── **NARRATIVE** ────────

| *Page* | *Section* | *Subject* |

──────── PART FOUR (cont.) ────────
Human Geography

APPENDICES

Contents

---------------------------------- MAPS & DIAGRAMS ----------------------------------

Page   *Figure*   *Subject*

------------------------------------ PART FOUR (cont.) ------------------------------------
Human Geography

LOCATION

N

W   E

S

SOUTHAMPTON

SOLENT

PORTSMOUTH

GOSPORT

SPITHEAD

LYMINGTON

COWES   E. Cowes

Fishbourne   RYDE

Seaview

St. Helens

Lat. 50° 41'N

Hurst
Point

Shalfleet

Yarmouth

NEWPORT

Totland

Freshwater

Calbourne

Bembridge

Brading

Arreton

SANDOWN

Shorwell

Brighstone

Godshill

SHANKLIN

Chale

VENTNOR

Niton

0	5	Kms
2	4	Miles

Long. 01° 18'W

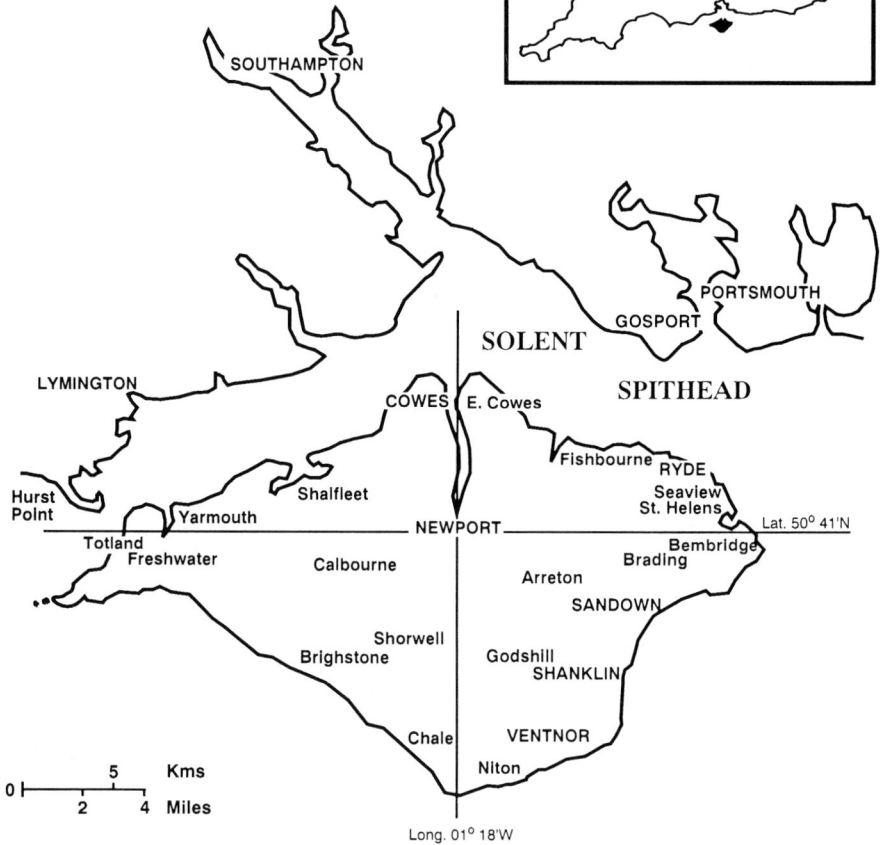

E N G L I S H   C H A N N E L

Fig 1. Position of the Isle of Wight

14

PART ONE

Introduction

1. LOCATION

"Where is it?", "How big is it?", etc.

(a) If you examine a map or globe of the World and search around Latitude 50 degrees 41 minutes North and Longitude 01 degrees 18 minutes West - there lies the centre of this beauteous Island, to the south of the British Isles and to the north of the English Channel. It is shaped like a diamond or lozenge.

(b) On the Ordnance Survey (O.S.) National Grid, the reference of Newport, its capital town, is - SZ 500890.

(c) A closer look will show that from East to West it is 37.8 kms (23.5 miles), North to South 22.5 kms (13.75 miles).

(d) Around the coastline is a distance of approximately 98.4 kms (60 miles).

(e) It has an area of 380.21 sq.kms (146.8 sq.miles) or 38.02 hectares (93,931 acres).

2. NAME

"How did it become "WIGHT"?

It is believed to have originated as "YNVS yr WYTH" ("The Isle of the Channel") but to the early Saxons it was called WHITLAND or WIHT-EA and, later, it may have been called by the Celtic "ICTIS" (not to be confused with St. Michael's Mount) in about B.C.85.

The Romans took possession around A.D.43 and called it "VECTIS" (from which many I.W. Companies take their name today); variations of the ancient names such as VECTA, WECHTS, WIHT and WHIT eventually led to the English name of "WIGHT" as we now know it.

As with the name of the I.W. so many names of Island towns and villages have altered over the years since they were first recorded in the Domesday Book.

Lastly, on this subject of names, if you hail from across the water we "Caulkheads" hope you "Overners" will enjoy your geographical exploration of this interesting isle.

PART TWO
Simple Geology of the I.W.

3. EARLY BEGINNING

"How did it get like this?"

The Island's history really begins not with its people but with its *rocks*. The best place to begin study of the geology of the I.W. is probably in Sandown Bay where the bones of huge reptiles can still be found in the *Wealden* clays which, like all rocks in the I.W., were laid down - layer upon layer - as a *sedimentary* rock under water, probably a shallow lagoon, dating back nearly 140 million years ago.

Also, in these ancient rocks, are many plant remains and, at Hanover Point (near Brook), the remains of an interesting petrified fossil log jam can be seen at low tide - where the early trees have turned into a form of *lignite*: this can also be found in, both, Alum Bay and Whitecliff Bay: the only places to find "coal" in the I.W.!

Since then, the whole area we now know as the I.W. has been covered by sea water, huge rivers or lakes and risen up again no fewer than seven times: examples of how the island mass has sunken and risen again are illustrated by the *raised beach* at Bembridge and the *marine gravel* laid down on the bottom of the Pliocene Sea but now found on top of Chillerton Down (see Fig 11) some 167 metres (548 feet) above sea level. At present it is thought to be sinking again - all of which can be more readily understood by a visit to the I.W. Museum of Geology. Here, can be found evidence of the actual fossils of Dinosaurs, Iguanadon etc., as well as huge ammonites and many other fascinating specimens. For over a decade an Indian Professor could be seen just under Culver Cliff in Sandown Bay, each Summer, searching - very successfully, for fossils in the Wealden clays.

Look at the Table (Fig 3) to follow the succession of rocks (from the bottom upwards) and at the Geological Map (Fig 2) to show where the main rocks *outcrop*; the I.G.S. "Special Sheet" is preferred for the more serious student which also shows the depth of each strata.

GEOLOGY

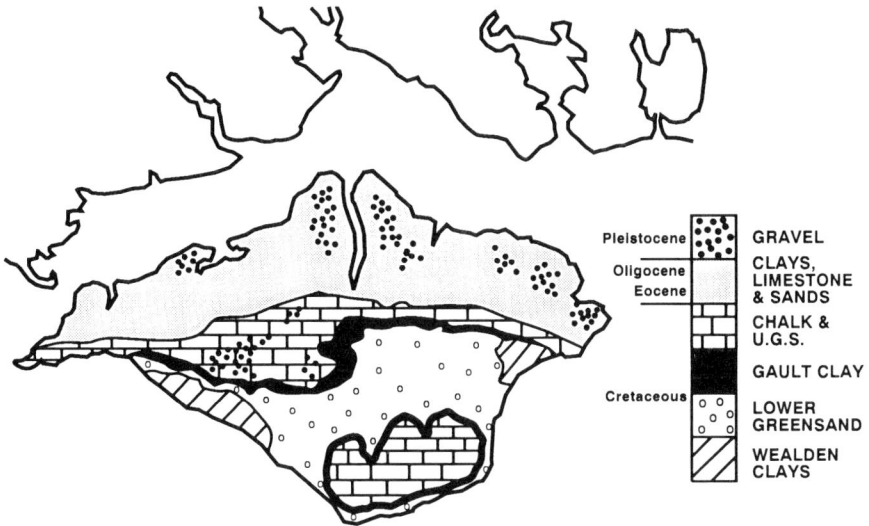

Fig 2. Simple Geology

Age		Period	Era	Rocks/Types	Formed of/from		Examples in I.W.
Mill	Yrs						
0			Recent	Alluvium			River Valleys
	2		Pleistocene	Gravels	Shallow sea		High Downs
35		PALAEOGENE		Clays L/S	Lakes, marshes	NORTHERN	Bembridge
			Oligocene	Sands	Lagoons		
				Clays	Shallow seas		Headon Hill
			Eocene	Sands/Clays	River Delta		Alum Bay
	54			Clays	Swamps		Newport
65		CRETACEOUS	Upper	Chalk & L/S	Shallow sea	SOUTHERN	E-W across I.W.
				Sands (U.G.S.)	Shallow sea		
				Gault Clay	Shallow sea		Shanklin
				(Blue slipper)			
			Lower	Sands (L.G.S.)	Shallow sea		Arreton
				Wealden Clays	Lagoons		Sandown Bay
	140				Marshes		S.E. Wight

Fig 3. Simplified Table of Strata

Over an immense period of time (look at the Age column in Fig 3) huge deposits of *chalk* were being laid down at a rate of about 2.5 cm (1") per 2,500 yrs; the depth of the chalk thus indicates a deposit period of over 50 million years. On top of this other layers of *sand, clays* and *gravels* have been deposited, some of which have been tilted giving near vertical sections and which can be seen as coloured rocks at both Alum Bay (Fig 4) and Whitecliff Bay.

This tilting of the rocks was caused by incredible pressures within the Earth's crust which led to a gigantic buckling of all the bedded layers of rocks - at a time when the Alps mountains were formed some 22 million or so years ago. From this *Folding* about 644 kms (400 mls) away the ripples led to the uplifting of what is known as the "backbone of the I.W." and which divides the Island into two distinct geological parts - *Cretaceous* - in the south and *Palaeogene* in the northern half - with a variety of *drift* deposits on top.

Study of the Island's rocks reflect the changing environment and once the sedimentary process was completed some 35 million years ago there began a further build up of these *drift deposits* of the more geologically recent *Pleistocene* period which, aside the high *relief*, defined much of the shape of the Island.

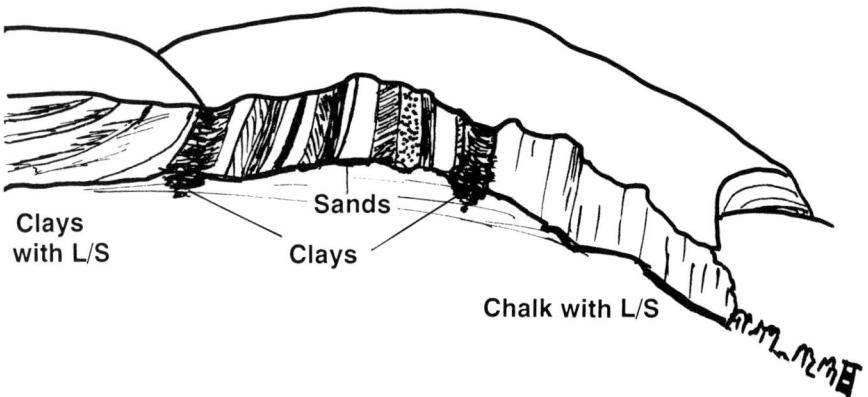

Fig 4. Field Sketch - Alum Bay, (to show near vertical strata).

18

PART THREE
Physical Geography

4. FOLDING

When the Earth's crust is *folded* masses of *horizontally bedded* sedimentary rocks (some of great thickness) are pushed up creating *anticlines* and down to form *synclines* (see Fig 5 over). Because of *erosion* the crest of an anticline is often exposed, showing the underlying rocks; clearly, the layers furthest down are the oldest rocks and those on top are the youngest (Fig 6).

In the I.W. the "rippling effects", mentioned in section 3, created anticlines and synclines which are named and shown in the map of the I.W. known as *GEOLOGICAL STRUCTURE* (Fig 7).

5. FIELD STUDY

"Where can we see all this?"

On the O.S. Map find the Quarry on Brading Down (Ref. 602867). There, if you look closely towards the west you will see a number of lines of flint in the quarry face, going in a parallel direction \ \ \ \ which is known as the *angle of dip*. On checking with the I.G.S. Geological Map, these are found to be at an angle of 85 degrees to the north.

Similarly, visits to Appuldurcombe (535804) and, across the water to Portsdown Hill (635065) would show the angle of dip, of all three as follows:

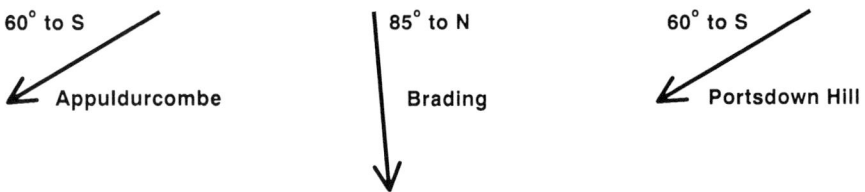

60° to S / Appuldurcombe   85° to N Brading   60° to S / Portsdown Hill

Now, by joining these (actual) lines of dip, as in the section over (Fig 8), it is possible to follow the trend of the shape of the land as was first formed millions of years ago. Since then the sea has flooded into

19

PHYSICAL - Folding

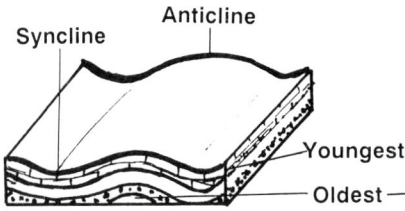

Syncline Anticline
Youngest
Oldest

Fig 5. Sketch - Folding

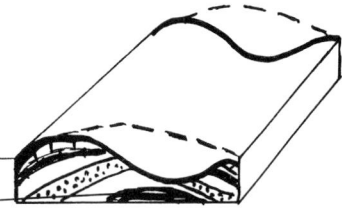

Youngest
Oldest

Fig 6. Sketch - Eroded Anticline

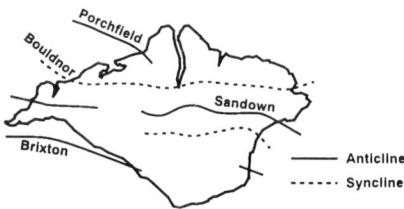

Porchfield
Bouldnor
Sandown
Brixton

—— Anticline
----- Syncline

Fig 7. Sketch Map - to show Geological Structure (axes of folding)

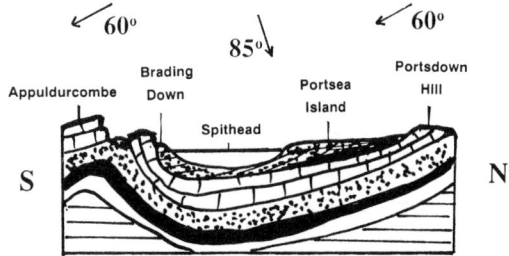

60°   85°   60°

Appuldurcombe   Brading Down   Portsea Island   Portsdown Hill

Spithead

S   N

Fig 8. Field Sketch section - across I.W. - Hants.

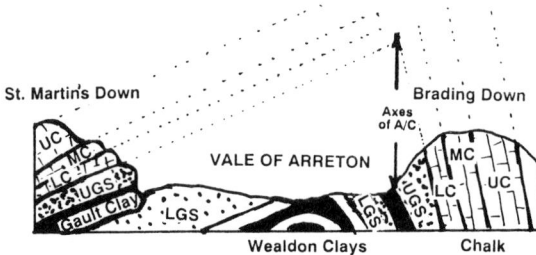

St. Martin's Down   Brading Down

Axes of A/C.

UC   MC   VALE OF ARRETON   MC
LC   UGS   LC   UC
Gault Clay   LGS   UGS
                              Chalk

Wealdon Clays

Fig 9. Field Sketch Section - across VALE OF ARRETON

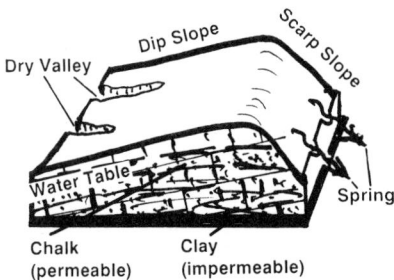

Dry Valley   Dip Slope   Scarp Slope

Water Table

Spring

Chalk (permeable)   Clay (impermeable)

Fig 10. Sketch - A "Cuesta"

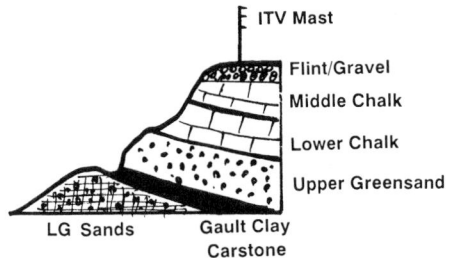

ITV Mast

Flint/Gravel
Middle Chalk
Lower Chalk
Upper Greensand

LG Sands   Gault Clay
            Carstone

Fig 11. Field Sketch Section - Chillerton Down

the syncline (Spithead) and the huge mountain (probably well over 1,500 metres or, nearly 5000 feet) that once formed the Sandown anticline has (after the land sinking and rising again) been eroded to provide the lovely *Vale* of Arreton and its underlying fertile rocks (Fig 9). This area, incidentally, has the highest average light intensity in the British Isles.

The above suggested field exercise is but one introductory sample of what you can see for yourself - following the well known precept that **"Real Geography is learned through the sole of one's boots!"**

There are many more opportunities for field studies in the I.W.; for example, regarding the geological nature of this part of the book:-
(a) How many "cuesta" can you find? What do they tell us about this particular part of the Island?
or (b) Why not find out about some of the other rock formations by making field sketches or drawings such as those in Fig 10 and 11 opposite?
Also, see "NOTES ON FIELDWORK" at the end of the book. (Appendix III).

6. RELIEF AND STRUCTURE
By starting our geographical enquiries with the Island's underlying rocks we can now begin to build up a picture which shows how the Geological *Structure* closely relates to the *RELIEF* or shape of the land surface of the I.W. above sea level. See Fig 12 over.

Clearly, the *hardest* rock in the I.W. is made of *chalk* and, by looking again at Fig 2 (Geology map), this leads us to the *highest* land along the central ridge (or "Backbone of the I.W."). The opposite is true of the *softest* rocks where lies the *lowest* land.

Equally, if we examine the coastline we find that the *headlands* and *cliffs* comprise the harder rocks and the *bays* the softest.

The principal *topographical* feature i.e. the lateral central ridge, is on an East-West axis of approximately 495 metres (1,500 ft) in thickness which outcrops at the surface to heights between 99 m (300 ft) at Downend and reaches its greatest *altitude* of 231 metres (700 ft) at

PHYSICAL - Relief & Structure

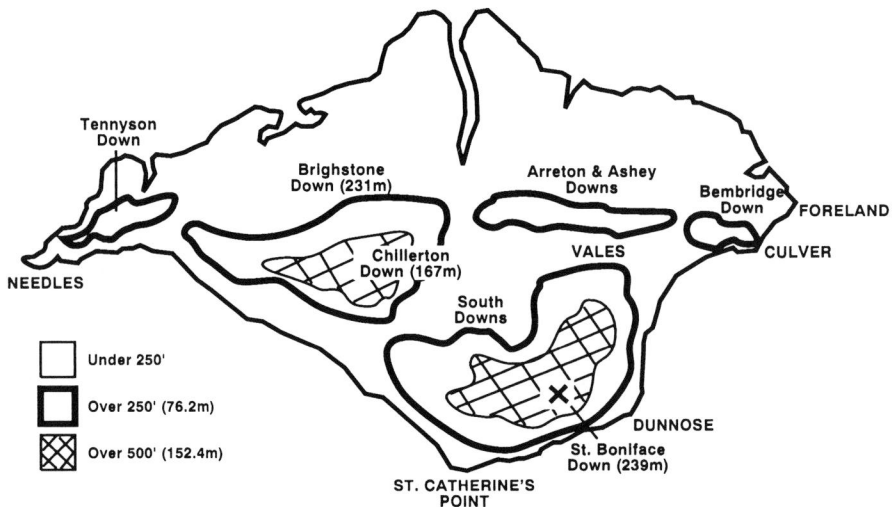

Fig 12. Sketch Map - I.W. Relief

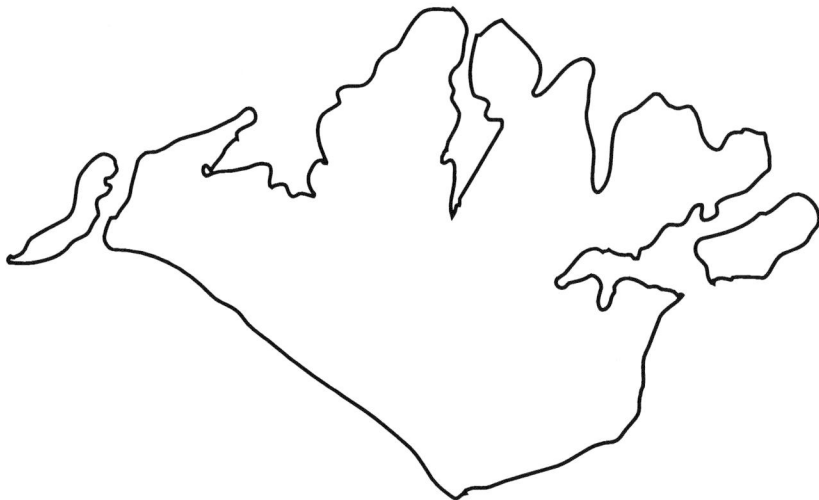

Fig 13. The "Isles" of Wight - in 3,000 A.D.?

Brighstone Down. It is broken by the smaller river W. Yar at Freshwater Bay but with much larger *river gaps* where the rivers Medina and E. Yar flow through.

Whilst the northern part of the Island is irregular lowland, on the south side of the Central Downs the "Bowl of the Island" contains the Vales of Arreton, Sandown and Newchurch broken up by ridges and rolling hills.

Below these the South Downs (a *scarped* part of the original Sandown anticline) rise to the highest point in the I.W., at St. Boniface Down 239 m (787 ft). The Downs throughout are *dissected* by a series of *dry valleys* although, on the south side of the South Downs, the rocks overlying the Gault Clay (or "Blue Slipper" as it is commonly known) tend to slide outwards towards the sea, producing *landslips* and *terraces*.

"Slipping" is not confined to the coast however and subsidence has occurred inland in many places where a *permeable rock stratum* rests on top of an *impermeable* one which becomes wet and slippery, especially at times of exceptional rainfall.

7. EROSION

Although we shall look at many of these problems later in the book, suffice to note that - ALL THE TIME, every day and night, even NOW as you read this, the shape of the land is changing. In the case of erosion or "wearing away" the surface is affected by *weathering* and the coast by *marine* action as the sea steadily pounds the shore coastline which in some instances is being eaten away by anything between 1 to 7.6 metres (3 to 25 feet) in a year; *landslips* of some 8 metres (26 feet) can occur in just one Winter.

Add it all up and you'll see that the I.W. is slowly shrinking as well as sinking and, by the year 3,000 A.D. could well become the

"ISLES" OF WIGHT

and look like the map opposite (Fig 13) which is also referred in Appendix IV.

RIVERS

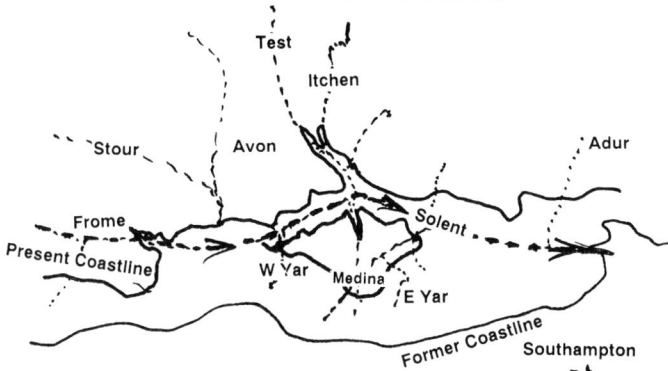

Fig 14(a).
Possible
drainage
pattern of
the area at
end of the
last Ice Age

Test

Itchen

Stour   Avon   Adur

Frome   Solent
Present Coastline
            W Yar Medina
                        E Yar
                Former Coastline
                        Southampton

Chichester

Fig 14(b). Former Chalk   Bournemouth
Ridge - breached by the sea
and, thus separates the I.W.
                        Isle of
                        Purbeck   Chalk

Alluvial Deposits in
drowned valley

Estuary   Flood Plain
                                        'Canalised' Section
                                        River Mouth
                                        Sluice
W. Yar   Medina   E. Yar

                                        River 'Capture' Area

Source   'Catchment' Area &
                                        Drainage 'Basin'

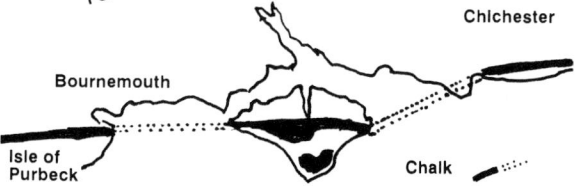

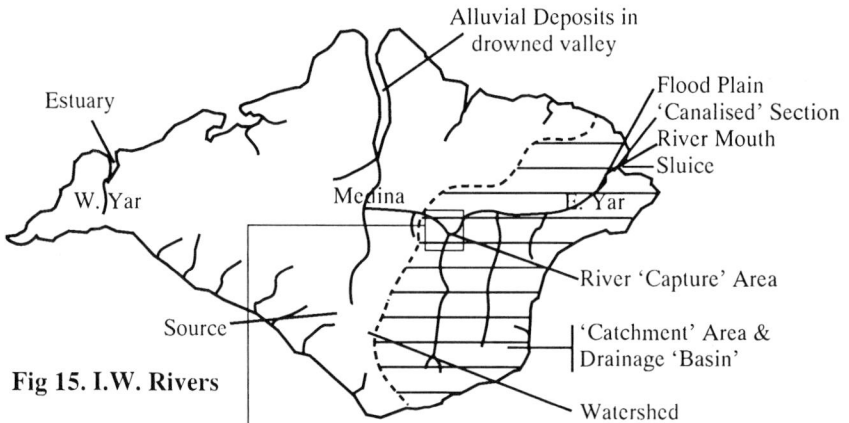

Fig 15. I.W. Rivers   Watershed

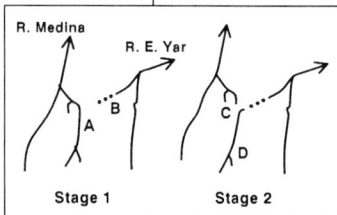

R. Medina
        R. E. Yar
                            NOTE
            B   A. Course of R. Medina tributary
        A   B. Headwaters of R. E.Yar 'cutting
                    C   back'
                    D   C. Elbow of River Capture
Stage 1   Stage 2   D. Former tributary of R. Medina has
                                now been 'captured' by R. E.Yar

Fig 16. Sketch diagram to show River Capture by E. Yar,
near Little Kennerley

8. RIVERS

Why do they all flow to the North?

The story of the Island's rivers begins long before the Wight became an island. Many million years ago the former "Solent River" (Fig14(a)) was fed by *tributaries* flowing north from over the huge anticlines of what we now know as the I.W. The *run-off* waters flowing steadily northwards *cut down* through the chalk rock, creating large *gaps* whilst, to the south, the streams ran across land now submerged and into the waters of the English Channel. The process of erosion went on non-stop and the *river gaps* in the Downs (at Yarmouth, Newport and Brading) grew larger and larger.

Then, after the last of the Ice Ages and as the climate grew warmer, the huge volumes of melting ice caused the sea level to rise until, eventually, the chalk ridge then existing W - E across from Purbeck was cut through by the sea which invaded the valley previously occupied by the former "River Solent". (Fig 14(b)).

Now, the original river tributary streams became the Island's own rivers - West YAR, MEDINA and East YAR - all flowing north! Or, to the more discerning student, the *subsequents* now became their own *consequents* - see Glossary for explanation if you are not sure.

Taking each of the Island's rivers in turn:-

(a) *River West Yar*

Must initially have been very, very much larger and longer (it has been estimated that in A.D.1 its headwaters were probably at least one mile further south) but it has since been cut off or *truncated* by marine erosion. Between its *source* and *mouth*, a distance of 3.4 km (2.5 mls), it falls less than 6.6 m (20 feet).

(b) *River Medina*

Rises near Chale at the base of St. Catherines Down, flows north to Newport where it is joined by the LUKELY BROOK at the head of the *estuary* after which it becomes *tidal*. It is 17 km (10.5 mls) long with a *catchment area* of 71 sq.kms (27.5 sq.mls). It is of interest that some of the earlier *headwaters* of the R. Medina have been diverted to the R. East Yar, S.W. of Merston by what is called *"River Capture"* (Fig 16). The R. Medina is still used by small vessels, up to 8 kms (5 miles) above its *mouth*.

(c) *River East Yar*

Rises near Niton also as a *spring* from St. Catherines Down. It flows north and on turning N.E. is joined by two major *tributaries* WROXALL STREAM and SCOTCHELLS BROOK before passing through a large gap at Brading. Thence, it flows across reclaimed land (formerly "Brading Haven" - see later) and, after passing through a "canalised" section - between flood banks, it finally outfalls at St. Helens through *tidal sluices.* In the winter its lower *flood plain* extends over nearly 610 hectares (1,500 acres).

It is 22 kms (13.5 miles) long and drains an area of about 70 sq.kms (34.5 sq.mls). It has been calculated that the water flow into the harbour at Bembridge averages approximately 60 megalitres per day - about 13,200,000 gallons.

9. SPRINGS

Where water passes through a *permeable* rock (e.g. Chalk) lying on top of an *impermeable* rock (e.g. Clay) it flows out of the ground as a *Spring*; in the I.W. we have large *Water tables* inside our *pervious* (permeable) rocks (Fig 10) some of which emerge on a *Spring Line* at places, (called Spring Line Settlements) such as Brighstone, Mottistone, Shorwell, Chillerton, Gatcombe etc. and are referred to under "Settlements" later in the book.

10. CHINES

Particularly along the S.W. coast, the south-flowing streams and rivulets make a hurried fall to the shore, down through mini ravines which, in the I.W., are called *Chines* (Fig 17). This name is derived from the Anglo-Saxon CINU or CINE meaning a cleft or fissure.

Perhaps the most famous include, on the S.E. coast, the chines at Shanklin and Luccombe; on the southern tip, at Blackgang and, further west, Whale, Shepherds, Grange, Shippards and Compton chines.

As a river flows, it cuts down, it cuts back and it cuts side-ways: hence, these mini canyons which are cut in a softer rock tend to widen and deepen over a very short distance; their side walls are smoothed by *wind erosion.*

CHINES & LANDSLIPS

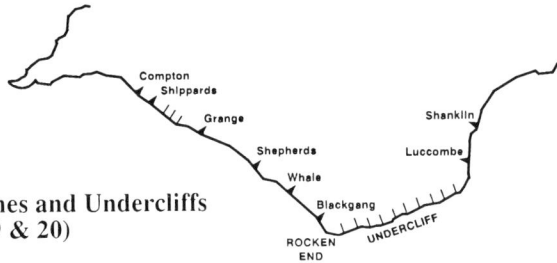

Fig 17. Location of Chines and Undercliffs
(see Figs 19 & 20)

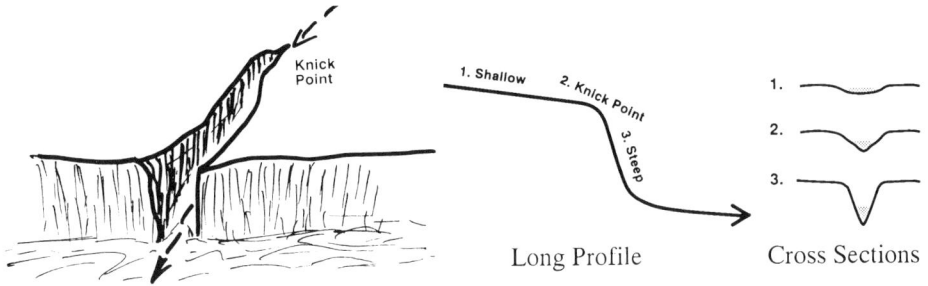

Long Profile

Cross Sections

Fig 18. Chines - Formation

Fig 19. Diagram to illustrate Rotational Slipping - Landslips

Fig 20(a). Landslides (e.g. Blackgang)

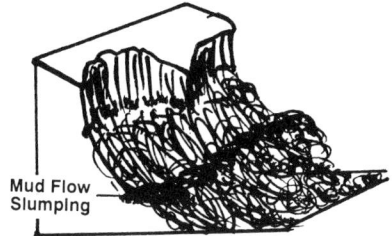

Fig 20(b). Slumping (e.g. Rocken End)

A chine contains a *rejuvenated* stream in a narrow valley, brought about by the rapid erosion of the cliff coastline; it is caused by:-
(a) change in base level and
(b) severe cliff recession.

The gentle gradient of the original stream reaches the *Knick Point* at the junction of the change to a much steeper gradient - where the stream enters the chine. This change occurs because the mouth of the rivulet is *truncated* by the sea cutting the cliff back faster than the river can cut its bed (Fig 18).

Where the old river bed *meander* has been completely cut off by the retreating cliff, this leaves a Dead Chine.

11. LANDSLIPS

The "Undercliff" between Shanklin and Blackgang is a splendid example of a *Landslip*, where a succession of short *escarpments* can be found at different levels. Many others are also found in the I.W. as at Luccombe, Bonchurch and between Ventnor and Niton. They are best illustrated in Fig 19 from which it can be seen that the Gault clay acts as a lubricant on which the Upper Greensand (U.G.S.) and Chalk are slipping - aided by their *dip* to the south.

12. SOILCREEP & "SLUMPING"

Exceptional rainfall (Sub-aerial erosion) can create both *Landslides* (not to be confused with Landslips) and "Slumping" - see Fig 20, both inland (e.g. on the sides of St. Catherines Down) as well as on the coast (e.g. particularly at Rocken End) where the position is aggravated by continued *Marine erosion* (attack by the waves) which quickly removes the fallen debris and clears the way for renewed activity. In some places the sodden clay flows like a "river of mud"; where this occurs inland and outpouring is not swept away by the sea, as at Winston, this flow can extend for many hundred yards.

13. WAVES

Waves are caused by winds (Fig 21). When a wave reaches shallow water around the coast its top falls forward and it is thrown up the beach shore (Fig 22). The breaking wave is called the *swash*; when it runs back

WAVES, BEACHES & COASTLINE

Little Wind

Little Waves

Strong Gale

High Waves

Fig 21. Wave patterns at sea

Swash
Backwash   Beach

Fig 22. Waves meet the shore

Fig 23. Longshore Drift (how material is carried along a beach)

Fig 24. Groynes (note pile on one side)

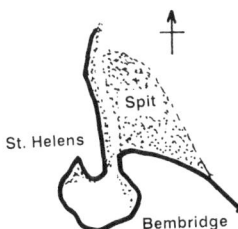

Spit

St. Helens

Bembridge

Fig 25. Spit forms across entry to harbour

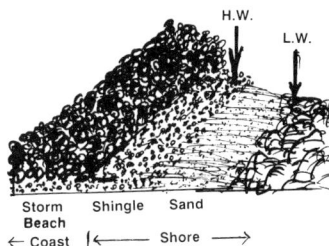

H.W.   L.W.

Storm   Shingle   Sand
Beach
← Coast | ←——— Shore ——→

Fig 26. Beach

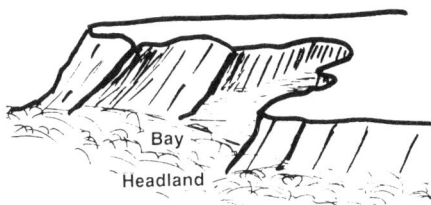

Bay
Headland

Fig 27. Typical I.W. scenery

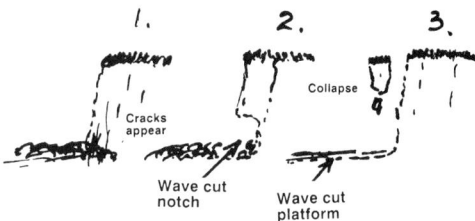

1.   2.   3.

Collapse

Cracks
appear

Wave cut
notch

Wave cut
platform

Fig 28. Cliff Erosion - stages

Caves   Arch   Stack

Fig 29. Cliff erosion - formation of Caves, Arches and Stacks

down the beach it is called the *backwash*. The flow of water from each wave moves up the beach, carrying its *load* (minute particles) at an angle (Fig 23) although the return flow, or backwash, aided by gravity allows the particles to run down again, at right angles; in turn, each wave repeats the action and so, as at the beach at St. Helens, you can see the result - called *Longshore Drift*. This can be reduced by building *Groynes* (Fig 24). Note the difference in height of the beach material on either side of the groyne.

Wave action *depositing* pebbles, mud and sand along the coasts of the I.W. helps to form gentle sloping beaches although some material carried along the coast - especially across river mouths (e.g. at Bembridge) is often deposited as a *Spit*. (Fig 25).

14. BEACHES

Nearly all the Island's southern beaches are sandy with a few, rather more pebbly or muddy, on the northern side. Most beaches lie between *High Water (H.W.)* and *Low Water (L.W.)* levels, as in Fig 26, but storm waves sometimes throw pebbles well up a normal sandy, shingly beach producing a long terraced ridge of larger shingle, called a *storm beach*. It is interesting to see and note how the size of beach particles are *graded*.

The "raised beach", at Forelands, Bembridge, some 15 metres (50 feet) O.D referred to in section 3, earlier, may possibly be part of the remnants of the southern shore of the former Solent River estuary.

15. COASTLINE

Except from Cliff End to the Needles, the whole northerly coastline is mainly shelving, low lying land with a number of creeks but few beaches. The more spectacular southern coasts, bounded by headlands and bays (Fig 27) provide most glorious scenery but, regrettably are steadily being worn away or broken by marine erosion.

Given the chance, the action of the sea everywhere is to straighten the coastline (hence the spit across the entry to the harbour at Bembridge). A rise in sea level along a lowland coast enables the sea to penetrate inland - "drowning" valleys and leaving marshes, swamps and mud flats in estuaries at low tide. Major "drowned" estuaries in the I.W. are to be found in the original Brading Haven, Newtown River and the Rivers W. Yar and Medina.

Serious cliff falls and erosion are constantly taking place as the sea attacks the southern coast; perhaps the most famous *STACKS* in the world - the **Needles** have been formed by this erosion which, with that of *CAVES, ARCHES, WAVE-CUT PLATFORMS* and *WAVE CUT NOTCHES* are illustrated in Fig 28 and Fig 29.

16. CREEKS AND HARBOURS

On the N.W. and N.E. coasts (see Fig 30) are to be found:-

(a) *Creeks* - largely for yachts and boats, at Yarmouth, Newtown River, River Medina estuary and Wootton (including the Ferry Terminal at Fishbourne).

(b) *Harbours* - both for commercial and recreational use, at Yarmouth, East & West Cowes, Newport and the man-made harbour at Ryde; also, at the eastern end of the Island, Bembridge Harbour - for which, see below.

All of which differ from each other and some of which are referred to in Part Four - the chapter on HUMAN geography.

17. BRADING HAVEN

How Man changes his environment!

Geography is concerned with the uniqueness of a given place and the interplay of all the factors which give it that special character. The following small study, primarily using maps, sets out to show how Man's efforts have changed one small corner of the I.W. over the years - what became of Brading Haven?

The story told by the maps:-

1. If we examine map extracts (a), (b) & (c) in Fig 31 over, we can see how the original spit in (a) was transformed into a mini *isthmus* or *peninsula* in (b).

2. Research has shown that this natural change probably occurred as the result of the "Great Storm" in 1703 when the outflow course of the R. East Yar was altered.

3. The map extract in (b) also shows the extent of the original "Brading Haven" and the Quay (still in evidence today) where

31

HARBOURS

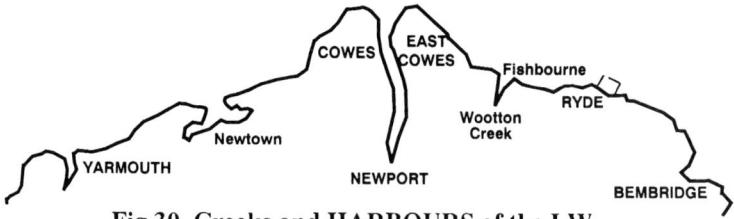

Fig 30. Creeks and HARBOURS of the I.W.

HOW MAPS CAN TELL A STORY

(a) 1611 (After Speed) (b) 1775 (Tracing Br. Museum) (c) 1880 (Sketch Map)

Fig 31. Map Extracts - Brading Haven and Bembridge Harbour

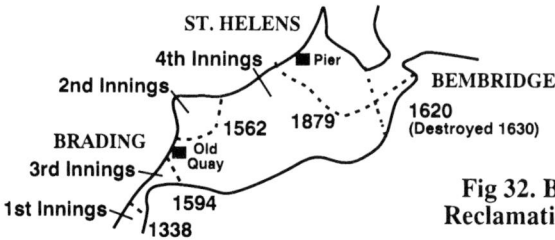

Fig 32. Brading Haven - Reclamations (or 'innings')

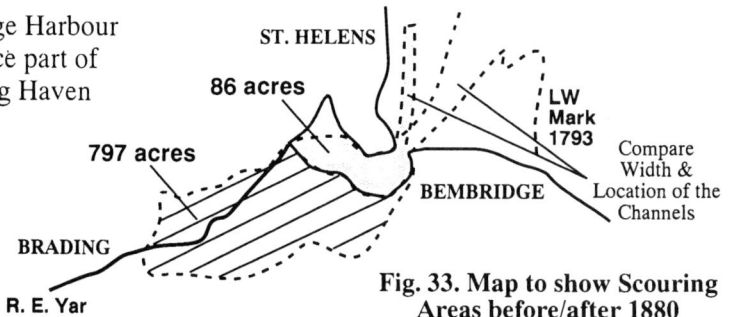

Bembridge Harbour was once part of Brading Haven

Fig. 33. Map to show Scouring Areas before/after 1880

history records the landing of King Charles II in 1665 and, before that, the area where the Romans landed from their galleys in about A.D.43. It will be seen that, from the earliest times Brading Haven must have afforded one of the main channels of entry to the Island. It was very sheltered and its proximity to the central chalk ridge gave access to the ancient track across the I.W.

4. From Fig 32 we can see how the earlier Haven was reclaimed by successive "Innings" from 1338 onwards. At that time the Haven remained open to a depth of 2.7 metres (9 feet) at M.H.W.S. as far as Brading Quay.

5. In 1879 the embankment was built - to carry the railway line from Brading via St. Helens to Bembridge. Hence, from Fig 31 (c), we can now see how the larger Haven became the new but smaller Bembridge Harbour and, also, how the R. East Yar was canalised to accommodate its newly constructed exit via the *sluice gates*.

6. Thus, Brading was no longer able to function as a port, however small; it had lost its oyster beds and had now become a *stranded* town.

7. Meanwhile Fig 33 shows the extent of the loss of *scouring* action by the river as well as the steady move westwards of the harbour exit channel.

We now know that Bembridge Harbour is steadily *silting up*; the map extracts explained above help us to understand how this process began to worsen - by Man's own action.

18. SEA

In general the depth of the sea around the I.W. varies between 16 to 33 metres (9 to 18 fathoms) except in the Western Solent narrows where the *ebb* tidal current cuts through and deepens the channel. By contrast, there is a sandbank off Ryde that dries out occasionally long enough to enable a game of cricket to be played - surrounded by sea!

Fig 34 over, shows the main 10 fathom line (18.3 metres) - about 3.2 kms (2 mls) off shore, as well as other *soundings* (in *fathoms*) and the 20 fathom (36.6 m) line. **Note** the Nab Tower where ship's pilots are picked up and dropped.

Fig 35 over, illustrates the comparatively shallow Solent and, to give

SEA & TIDES

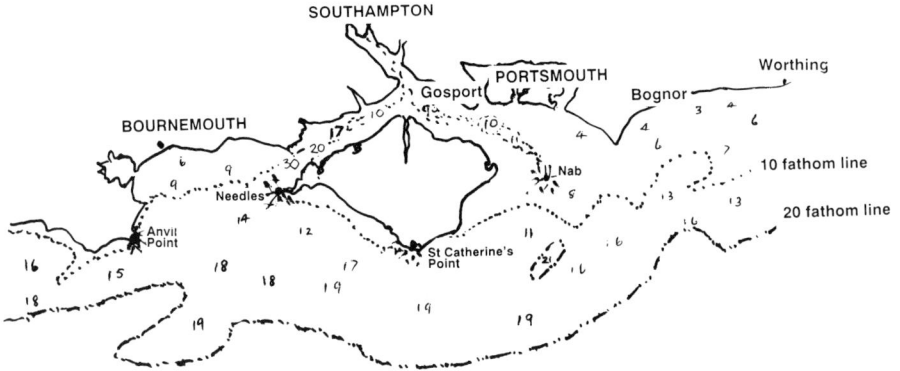

Fig 34. Sea Area around the I.W.

Fig 35. Between Portsmouth and Ryde (how far out of water - St. Pauls Cathedral

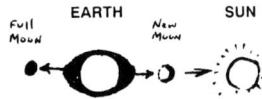

Fig 36. Spring Tides

Fig 37. Spring and Neap Tides (Ranges)

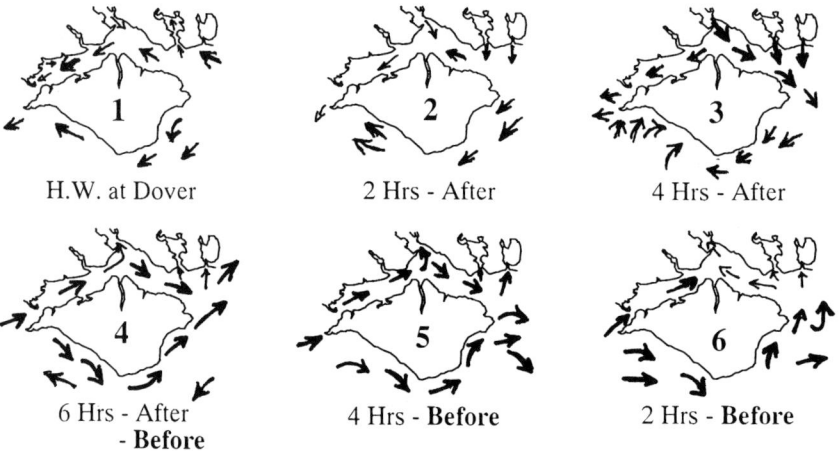

H.W. at Dover

2 Hrs - After

4 Hrs - After

6 Hrs - After - Before

4 Hrs - Before

2 Hrs - Before

Fig 38. I.W. Tidal Flows in relation to H.W. at Dover

some rough idea of the depth of the sea in this area, it suggests how much of St. Paul's Cathedral would be showing above the high tide if it were to be lowered temporarily in the middle of the sea between Ryde and Portsmouth!

19. TIDES

The rise and fall in sea levels around the coasts, known as *High* and *Low tides* is due to the gravitational pull of the moon and, to a lesser extent, the sun. When all are in a straight line this "pull" is at its greatest - see the sketch diagram (Fig 36).

When the moon is "full" or "new" is when the highest tides occur - these are called *Spring* tides; the opposite effect happens when the moon is pulling at right angles which leads to lower tides called *Neaps*. The difference between them is called the *tidal range* which, in the I.W. is around a maximum of 4.3 m (14 ft) at Spring tides and 1.8 metres (6 feet) at Neap tides (Fig 37).

Tidal flow charts are based on the times of H.W. at Dover, which are adjusted locally for each area. Inspection of Fig 38 should help to explain why tidal differences occur, at varying stages, between the east and west ends of the Island. For example, H.W. at Yarmouth occurs roughly one hour after H.W. at Ryde.

Another feature of benefit to the creeks and harbours on the north coasts of the I.W. results from the extended and prolonged build-up of tidal water in Southampton Water (often **wrongly** referred to as a "double high tide" or "four tides a day"). This build-up is maintained for two to three hours, twice daily, arising from a second flow of water up the inlet, whilst there is still slack water from the first.

"Tide Tables" can be purchased locally, giving the exact times of high and low water in a particular place, each day: always remember to adjust the times given, accordingly, when they are listed only in *Greenwich Mean Time* (G.M.T.).

20. WEATHER

Weather Stations are located in a few towns in the I.W. and some of their records are reported in the major national daily papers. A typical weather recording station, like that at Ventnor, is shown in Fig 39, opposite. From this it will be seen that various measurements are taken such as the wind speed and direction, max. and min. air temperatures, ground and soil temperatures, amount of rainfall and periods of sunshine. All these details are plotted regularly, over a long period of time and, from which, the many figures collected are used to compile *Weather Statistics*.

Some examples of these are as follows :-

SANDOWN	SUN(hrs)	RAIN	TEMP (Max)	GENERAL
Winter	0	.10cm	55°F	Rain
(24hrs.)		*.04in.*	*13°C*	
Summer	8.1	0	76°F	Sunny
(24hrs.)		*0*	*24°C*	

Annual total 1, 841.9 = Average **5.04 hrs per day**, over the year.

RYDE - *Rainfall* in Summer (May - Sept)- Records
Low 11.7 cms. (4.61 ins) (1940)   No. of rainy days 31 (1921)
High 41.2 cms (16.2 3ins) (1974)   82 (1954)
Temperature Ranges (Annual)
Max - by day varied between 13°C - 23°C
Min - by night 3°C - °8C
(Source data figures, from K.J. Hosking F.R. Met. S., Binstead I.W.)

All these various figures enable comparisons to be made between different places and for the same place in different years or at different times in the same year. Even in such a small island it is sometimes quite surprising to find such variations in the weather between the East and West of the Island and, likewise, North and South.

21(a). CLIMATE

Thus, it can be seen that the weather patterns are changing daily and all the time. Hence it is only by averaging out **all** the data collected over a much longer period of time that a more accurate summary picture emerges - this is the *climate*, partly illustrated in Fig 40 opposite.

The more mature student will note the correlation between the Relief (Fig 12) and the Rainfall. The *Isohyets* reflect the numerous polar front depressions which sweep across the I.W. In general, the Island's Climate can be summarised, in geographical terms as having:-

WEATHER

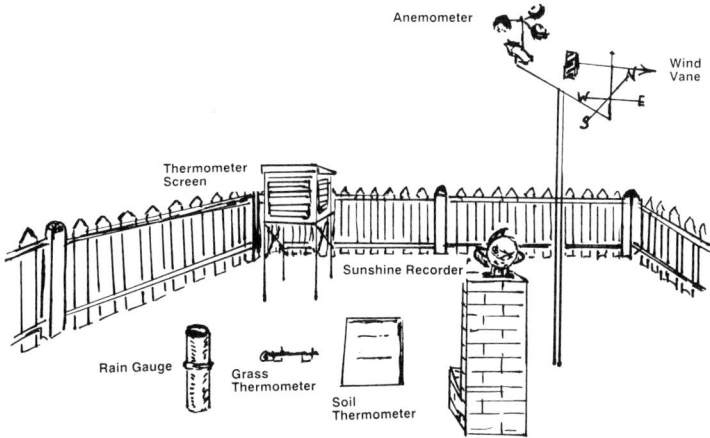

Anemometer

Wind Vane

Thermometer Screen

Sunshine Recorder

Rain Gauge

Grass Thermometer

Soil Thermometer

Fig 39. Sketch Diagram of a Weather Station

CLIMATE

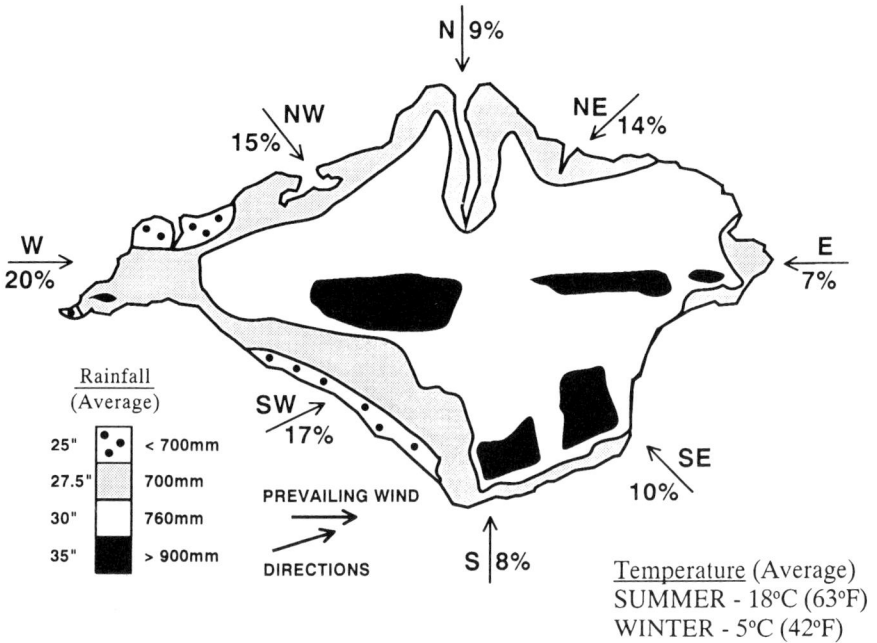

N 9%

NW 15%

NE 14%

W 20%

E 7%

SW 17%

SE 10%

S 8%

Rainfall (Average)

25"	< 700mm
27.5"	700mm
30"	760mm
35"	> 900mm

PREVAILING WIND

DIRECTIONS

Temperature (Average)
SUMMER - 18°C (63°F)
WINTER - 5°C (42°F)

Fig 40. Rainfall and Wind Direction

Warm Summers
Cool Winters
Moderate Rainfall - all year
} or, what, more technically
is known as Cool Temperate
Western Margin Type climate

RECORDS OVER MANY YEARS SHOW THAT THE ISLE OF WIGHT ENJOYS MORE SUNSHINE AND DAYLIGHT HOURS THAN ANY OTHER PART OF BRITAIN.

21(b). LAND AND SEA BREEZES

Along the I.W. coastline in the summer, the air moves from sea to land by day (an ON-Shore breeze) and at night from land to sea - (an OFF-Shore breeze); this is because the land gains and loses heat more quickly than the sea. This principle of warm air rising and being replaced by heavier colder air applies on a larger scale to the World's Wind Belts and to the Monsoons.

22. SOILS

All soils contain common elements (e.g. minerals, humus, air, water and living organisms) although the *Soil Profile* (Fig 41) in any one place is influenced by the actual balance of these minerals, organisms, water movement and, particularly the solid bedrock on which it lies.

The main rocks in the I.W. are CHALK, CLAY and SAND with some deposits e.g. *Loess* at St. Helens, *Peat* at Gatcombe and *Alluvium* in the R. East Yar flood plain.

Each type helps to determine the use to which it is put. Thus, on the *non-porous CLAYS* in the North we find pasture, ponds and woodlands while, on the central Downs, the *porous CHALK* gives rise to short rough grass, few trees and occasional Springs. On either side of the Downs and in the Bowl of the Island - often mixed *with clay* are the *SANDS* which form the more productive *loamy* soil.

23. LAND USE

The I.W. is fortunate in that most of its surface is covered by usable soil. Of the total 93,931 acres (38,012 ha) approximately 75% is agricultural land and around 11% forest; the balance is taken for *Urban* use (11%) and only the 3% remaining is derelict or despoiled land.

LAND USE

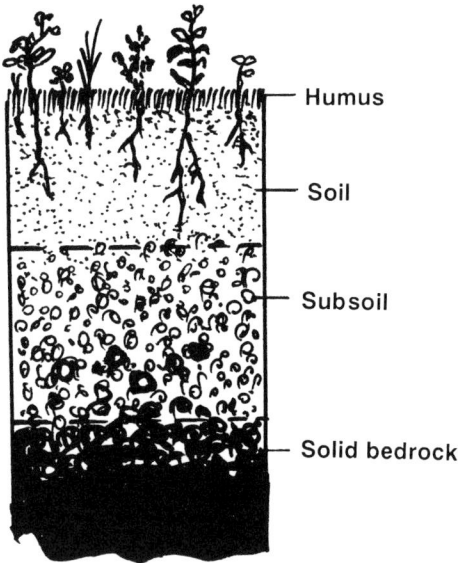

Humus

Soil

Subsoil

Solid bedrock

Fig 41. Soil Profile

Deciduous   Coniferous

Broad leaf   Needle leaf

Fig 42. Trees - Types

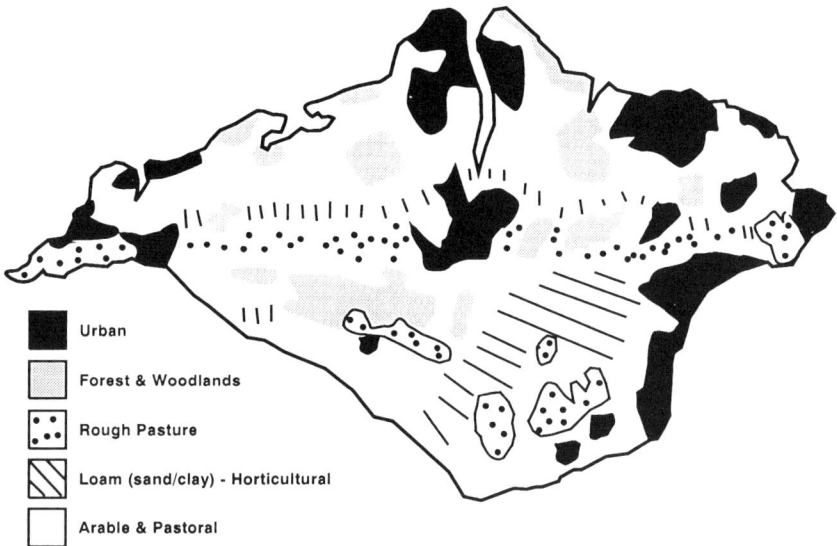

Urban

Forest & Woodlands

Rough Pasture

Loam (sand/clay) - Horticultural

Arable & Pastoral

Fig 43. Simple Sketch Map to outline Main Land Use

The quality and use of Land in the I.W. is shown, roughly, in Fig 43 which in addition to soil structure also takes the varying factors of climate and relief into account. See also Appendix II.

24. VEGETATION

The Island's vegetation is classified (see Section 22) and because of our minimum Winter temperatures for plant growth, this results in most of our trees shedding their leaves i.e. they are *Deciduous*, with broad leaves (Fig 42). Hence, our main Forests (at Parkhurst, Brighstone and Combley) reflect this pattern viz Beech, Oak, Ash etc., together with some *Coniferous* trees e.g. Pine, Fir etc., although several other species are to be found in the many other woodlands and copses, including Osier Beds.

25(a). NATURAL HISTORY

Habitats for plants and animals found in the countryside are largely determined by the underlying geological structure and the soils arising from this. In the I.W. the changing colours of these soils often provide a clue to the *Flora* and *Fauna*. The great diversity and change of these soils and environments, over a comparatively small area prompts a huge ecological interest, attended by exceptional I.W. representation of mammals, reptiles, amphibia and bird life.

25(b). ECOSYSTEMS

Currently, modern Geographers are increasingly studying *Systems* of relationships between, for example - plants, animals, soils, man and the atmosphere. If all the *cycles* in this complicated *network* of chemical, moisture and energy *flows* etc. are plotted out in a state of balance - so that it can be seen how the changes in one part effect the other parts - this is known as an *Ecosystem*.

———————— • ————————

This last section in the **Physical** Geography chapters introduces the nature and use of the land in the I.W. whereas the next, in the first part of the **Human** Geography division, shows what the Island farmers have done with it.

PART FOUR
Human Geography

26. INDUSTRY
Industry is usually classified into three groups:-
(a) **Primary** - extractive activities
(b) **Secondary** - manufacturing
(c) **Tertiary** - services

This first section deals with **PRIMARY INDUSTRIES IN THE I.W.**

27. AGRICULTURE
In earlier times the Island abounded in small fields and the main activity was **Farming** which employed large numbers of workers. Today, the scene has changed from a mass of small farm units to a modern and thriving industry where, thanks to efficient farm management and mechanisation, much higher yields are produced from the same land, by far fewer but more qualified people, in much larger holdings.

As the market changes so the growth of various crops and the farming of particular animals also alters; changes also come about as the result of political action (e.g. European Common Market). Thus, for the sake of current accuracy, exact figures of acreages given over to each crop, numbers of livestock animals or buildings, workers etc. have deliberately been omitted. However, since the climatic and soil conditions largely determine what can be grown and where (see sections 22 - 24) typical crops found in the I.W. are illustrated in Fig 44 over, as well as livestock in Fig 45. Look out for examples of *contour ploughing*, to prevent the rich soil at the top of a large, sloping field from being washed down to the bottom by heavy rain.

Apart from *Arable*, *Mixed* and *Dairy* farming, high light intensity levels in Winter in the Arreton Valley are ideal for *HORTICULTURE* and the growing of small vegetables and flowers under glass.

VITICULTURE (grape vines) is also carried on at the vineyards at Adgestone, Cranmore, Smallbrook and E. Cowes. *POULTRY* are kept and *specialised* crops such as sweetcorn and garlic are also grown.

41

ISLAND FARMING

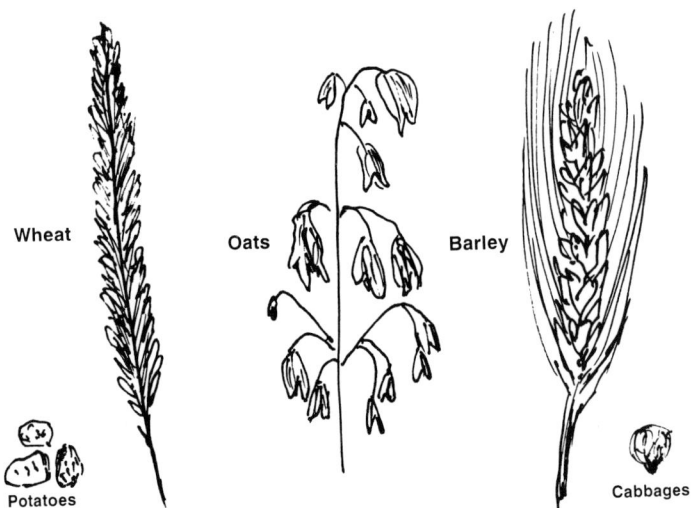

Wheat

Oats

Barley

Potatoes

Cabbages

Fig 44. Typical Arable Crops in I.W.

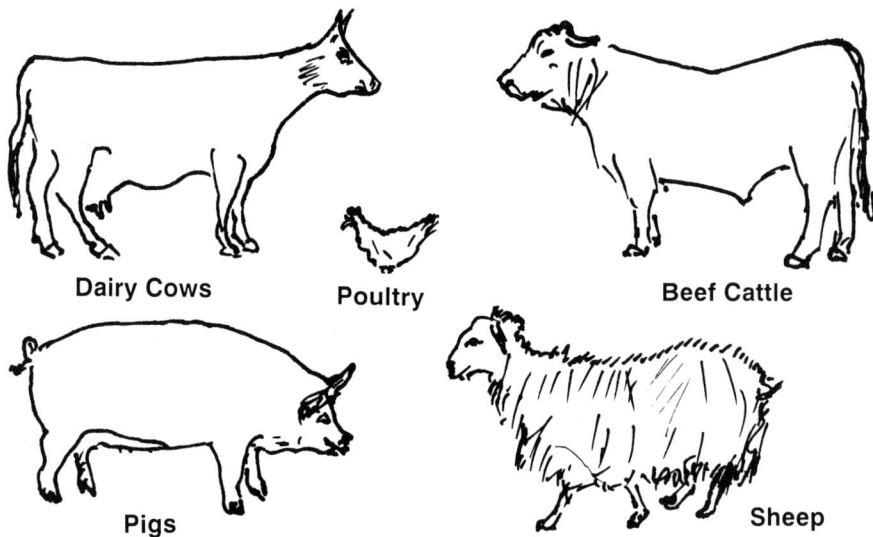

Dairy Cows

Poultry

Beef Cattle

Pigs

Sheep

Fig 45. Typical Livestock in I.W.

In the Spring, colourful areas of oilseed rape and linseed are to be seen. **Agriculture is an important primary industry in the I.W.**

28. OTHER PRIMARY INDUSTRIES

(a) *Forestry* - previously mentioned in section 24 some 60% of which is managed by the Forestry Commission.

(b) *Fishing* - Shellfish e.g. crabs and lobsters and Wet fish e.g. plaice, sole and cod are landed at Yarmouth, Freshwater Bay, St. Helens and Bembridge whilst oysters are gathered from Newtown Estuary.

(c) *Quarrying* - the I.W. was noted in the past for its freestone obtained from the Binstead and Ventnor areas but, unfortunately, they have now been worked out. This is true also of the extraction of clay for brickmaking since the works at Rookley (red and brown) and in E. Cowes (yellow bricks) are now closed. Examples of lovely old stonework are to be seen all across the Island including flint (e.g. Brighstone Church). Nowadays, the only minerals still worked on the I.W. are limestone, chalk, sand and gravels for the Construction industry.

29. SECONDARY INDUSTRY

As change has occurred in the Primary practice of farming over the last few decades so, even more, has been the case with Secondary (or *Manufacturing*) industries in the I.W. - but for different reasons.

This Island has a proud pioneering record and, in the past, great sailing ships and warships were built at Cowes, rockets at High Down, light aircraft at Bembridge and "Princess" flying boats at E. Cowes, all of which, today, are now writ in history: the major sole survivors among the larger companies being the hovercraft still at E. Cowes and the advanced electronic and radar equipment at Northwood.

Now, the Island has a broad range of other mainly smaller manufacturing industries (Fig 46) largely centred on Cowes, Newport and Ryde, in small *Industrial Estates* at Ventnor, Lake etc. as well as an ever-growing number of *Rural* and *Craft* (Fig 47) industries; indeed, even a few *Cottage* industries. See also Appendix II.

Clearly, manufacturing industry in the Island reflects the national

INDUSTRY

GAUGES.
GRP. H/C ENGINES.
PVC. ELECTRONIC RADAR.
OIL BOOMS. SAILS. PHOTO
COWES
PRINTS. TV PARTS.
GRP BOATS. MOULDINGS.
HANKIES BOATS
ELERT ENG.

WINE

WOOD CARVING.
COSMETICS. BOATS.
RYDE
SPORTS CLOTHING.
ELECT ENG. CAST WORK.
MASTS.

NAME PLATES.
CONCRETE PRODUCTS.
PLASTIC MOULDINGS. TIMBER
WORK. COACH LDG.
NEWPORT
AGRIC ENG. ART STONE.
ELECT ENG. FURNITURE
TENTS.

BOATS
TOTLAND &
FRESHWATER
SPRING
GRP. TOYS. KNITWEAR
CANDLES

ART STONE

BOATS. ENG.
A/C.
BEMBRIDGE
CROP SPRAY

WINE

OPTICAL. BLINDS.
ICE CREAM. GRP.
SANDOWN &
SHANKLIN
ELECT. TEL CABLE FITTINGS.
STATIONERY.
CANDLES

LOCKS.
POTTERY. CLOTHING
GRP. BOATS.
VENTNOR
GLASS.
FOODSTUFFS

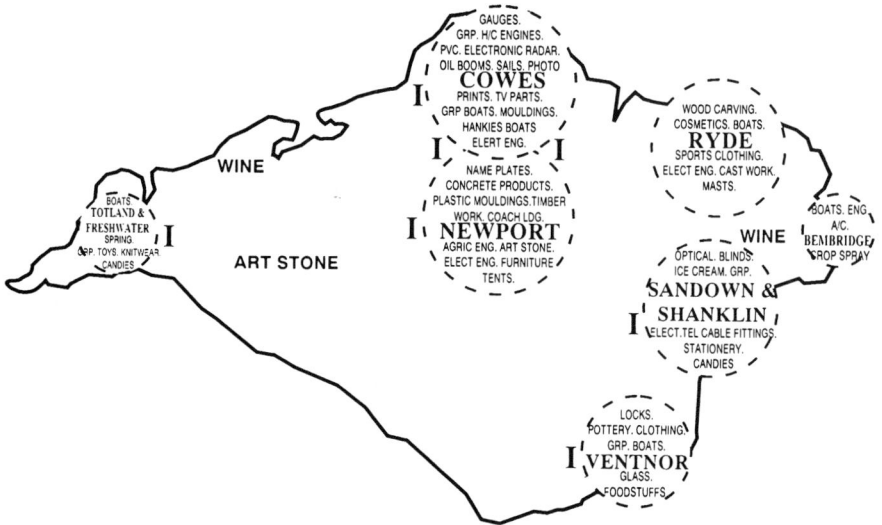

Fig 46. I.W. Manufacturing - some industries.
Note: I - Trade/Industrial Estates - see 35(d)

The Island is rich in its artists and craftsmen - their
works range from pottery, glass, jewellery to
wrought iron - and more!

Fig 47. Sign on the
Sandown/Newport Road

Fig 48. You'd be surprised by the great range of things made on the I.W.

move away from heavy industry and manual work - comparative figures show the trend to be greater in the I.W. Here, there are far fewer firms employing more than fifty people although a growing feature is the number of small *Light Industrial* concerns making a whole range of different things (Fig 48) with between two and nine employees.

As with change in the nature of industry so has change occurred in style. Thus, for example in the yacht and boat-building industry, the former large, wood constructed racing yachts, timber motor launches and smaller craft have now given way to *G.R.P.* (Glass, Reinforced Plastic) development; cotton sails have given way to nylon; inboard engines have in many cases been superseded by outboard engines and, in the world of competitive sailing, "class" boats are becoming ever smaller and varied (e.g. wind surfers).

No attempt has been made to name individual firms but several Island businesses continue to enjoy world renown. As a concluding comment - how many know that the world land speed record car, called **" THRUST 2"** was built at Fishbourne in the Isle of Wight? Let this example demonstrate that the Island's pioneering spirit in the industrial world , however small, remains of the highest order.

30. TERTIARY INDUSTRY

This name refers to the many commercial and other occupations providing a "service" to the public. In the I.W. this accounts for, by far, the greatest number of jobs such as banking, insurance, professional (e.g. Nurses), administrative etc. including that most important item of the Island's economy - **tourism** (see section 31). Again, "change" is the keyword and, so, here in the I.W. we see how the tertiary sector is continually on the move. For example, shopping habits have switched from the High Streets (where former retail shops have now become estate agents, betting shops etc.) to the out of town superstores, national companies (Marks & Spencers, Army & Navy, B.H.S. etc.) have moved into the I.W., local government operations have altered, more recreational centres have opened - which, with many other changes, all affect the lives of the Island people and are referred later in the book.

45

31. TOURISM

Because of its frequent occurrence as a topic in school and in examinations and, particularly, in the lives of all Islanders as well as the general economy of the I.W. this section is deliberately expanded and more closely investigated, under five headings.

(a) *Visitors and Holidays* - The writer has been fortunate enough to have circumnavigated the world and to have sampled many visits to different tourist areas in all the major continents. He has yet to find a more all-inclusive and varied Summer Holiday region than the ISLE OF WIGHT!

The criteria associated with Tourism as a major Tertiary industry are examined later; meanwhile, let us look at some of the answers given in response to an "A" level student's survey question, as follows:-

"Why is the I.W. one of the principal holiday centres in the U.K.?" Some replies included;-

"The Island as a whole is better than an individual resort.

You can enjoy a relaxing and quiet holiday if you want to.

It is good as a "second holiday" and for repeat visits.

It has the widest choice of accommodation and facilities.

There's so much for all the family to do - indoors and out.

There are good facilities for the disabled.

The people are so helpful and friendly.

It regularly tops the "sunshine charts" in the U.K.

There is beautiful country scenery inland and some healthy walking.

It is easy to get to the I.W. and by so many routes (and, by the same person, under).

As a holiday island it seems to have the romance of "going foreign".

We love the white cliffs and sandy beaches for the kids.

It was less expensive than we feared, except for the crossing by sea, when compared with the ferries to France.

I couldn't believe the number of boats in the "Round the Island" race - there were hundreds and hundreds.

We aren't culture hunters but there sure was much to see.

We came over for the day to see it all but reckon it would take us a month, flat out."

There were many other responses, not all so complimentary but, surprisingly, very few criticisms of any validity. These answers have been selected to give the opportunity for students to investigate (at first hand and then by *secondary source material*, such as this book or holiday literature) some of many components of the Holiday industry.

STUDENT EXERCISES
Thus, before moving on, here are two exercises :-

1. Make a full page copy of Fig 49, below. On this map, insert the names of:-

(i) all the Holiday Camps marked H.C.

(ii) all the other items shown in the Key, in their proper places.

2. Make LISTS to show:-

(i) as many *factors* of Tourism e.g. access, climate, facilities etc., etc. as you can and

(ii) in the case of the I.W., the Recreational and Leisure opportunities available, types of accommodation, sights to see, things to do and other factors.

How do your answers compare with Fig 50 and the paragraphs following?

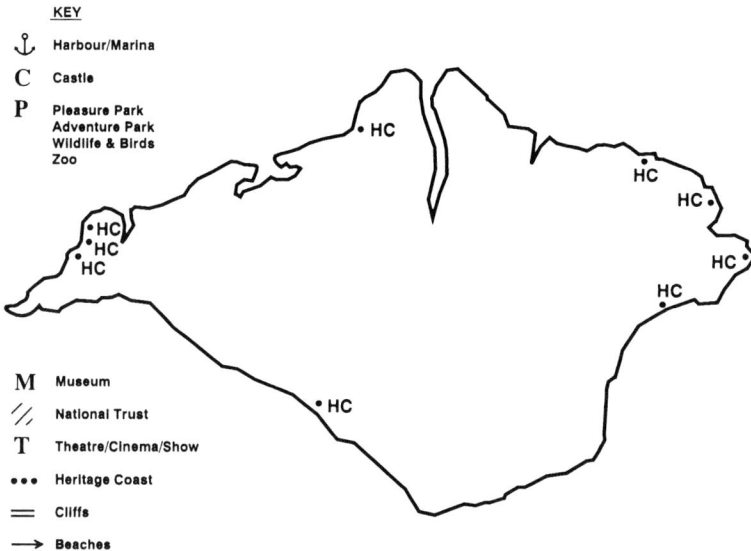

KEY

⚓ Harbour/Marina

C Castle

P Pleasure Park
Adventure Park
Wildlife & Birds
Zoo

M Museum

// National Trust

T Theatre/Cinema/Show

••• Heritage Coast

= Cliffs

→ Beaches

Fig 49. Quiz Map - I.W. Tourist Amenities?

TOURISM

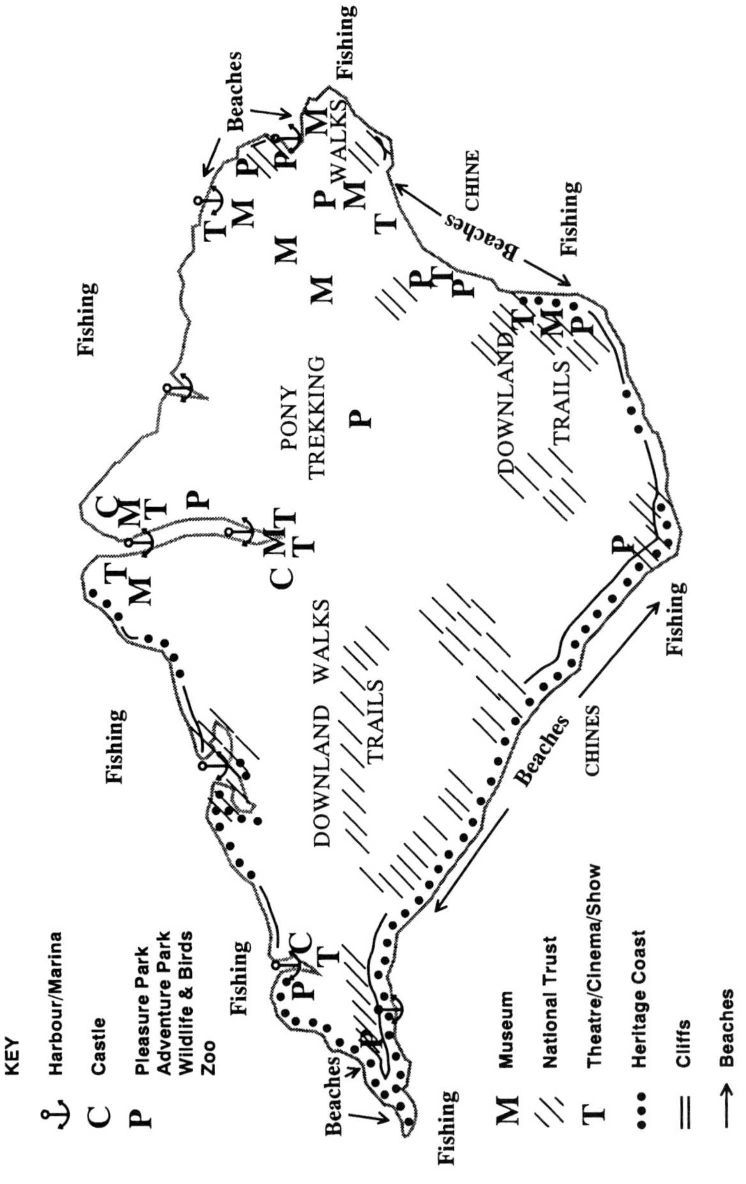

Fig 50. Sketch Map to show I.W. Tourist Amenities

KEY

⚓ Harbour/Marina

C Castle

P Pleasure Park
  Adventure Park
  Wildlife & Birds
  Zoo

M Museum

⁄⁄ National Trust

T Theatre/Cinema/Show

••• Heritage Coast

= Cliffs

→ Beaches

(b) ***Recreation and Sports*** - "Cowes Week", in August each year, is world renowned as the mecca for sailing enthusiasts. There are many other water sports in the I.W. as well - from swimming to surfing, jet skiing to power boat racing, canoeing to windsurfing, angling to deep sea fishing, numerous regattas and, for young children, simply paddling in the sea.

Gliding, flying, paragliding and hang gliding are all to be had for the outdoor ethereal enthusiasts whilst, indoors, ice-skating, ten-pin bowling, badminton, squash, dancing are all on hand plus, in the larger hotels and in a number of towns, heated indoor swimming pools. There are athletics stadia, cycling clubs, tennis courts, bowling greens, golf courses and cricket to watch or play; for those who enjoy walking, apart from the rambling clubs, there are miles of meandering coastal paths that circle the Island.

For those who love nature, there is an abundance of *Trails* giving opportunity for study of bird and animal life, a great variety of Nature Trails as well as some very interesting Long Distance Trails.

(c) ***Leisure Attractions*** (Fig 50) - These incorporate Theme Parks, historic buildings, craft centres, a zoo, wild-life parks, vineyards, glass and pottery making, band concerts, museums, art exhibitions, cinemas, theatres and music hall, pubs, clubs, country parks and manors, castles, steam trains, stone-age settlements, Roman villas, dinosaurs, carnivals, fireworks, bird parks, botanical gardens, visits to the homes of famous people from the past and, always, the fun of a "bucket and spade" on one of the many sandy beaches.

Touring in the Island is pleasurable itself - for example through the Undercliff area: each village has a charisma of its own, whilst the *spa town* of Ventnor contrasts with the commercial market and *County town* of Newport which is quite different from Cowes as a *Ferry port* or the varied *Holiday towns* of Ryde, Sandown and Shanklin.

(d) *Tourism in the I.W.* - A project set up recently by the International Federation of Tour Operators attempted to draw together the many parts that make up tourism into a *Model*. This model was based on three requirements for sustainable tourism:-

(i) that the resident population should keep its cultural identity, backed up by good integrated planning

(ii) that the tourist centre should remain clean and attractive to tourists

(iii) that nothing (*sic*) should be done to damage the ecology.

Monitoring such as the quality of life, maintenance of the environment etc. relies on *Behavioural Geography* but, on all three counts, the writer believes that the Isle of Wight would emerge from any enquiry with a high ranking score.

However, over the last twenty years or so, there has been a marked decline in the stock of hotels and bed-spaces available and there still remains a need to upgrade the levels of accommodation generally and to build a number of new Four and Five Star hotels if adequate provision is to be made for the needs of future holidaymakers and, above all, for first class *Conference* facilities which could be such a boon to the Island's economy. A higher standard of new-style "Theme Park" development would also add to the Island holiday image.

Tourism in the I.W. is a vibrant and buoyant industry central to the Island's economy and social well-being. As referred in the model project, it is a matter of fine balance how this is maintained without upsetting the indigenous population or damaging the natural beauty of the Island. Currently, the holiday industry operates in a highly competitive market during a limited Summer season; it needs to expand the length of season, increase its "off-peak" and "short-break" appeal and, for those accustomed to a main Continental holiday, develop a stronger "second holiday" role. At the moment relatively few visitors from abroad come to the I.W. which means loss of a valuable *Invisible Export*. Unlike many holiday centres the I.W. receives a high number of individual bookings beside the usual *"Package Holidays"*.

During the peak high season periods most of the ferries and all the accommodation available is being used to capacity; it follows therefore that figures showing numbers of tourists visiting the Island must remain stable at these times, which does not necessarily indicate any lack of growth over the rest of the year. It may be of interest to note a random sample of the origin of visitors coming to the I.W. (Fig 51) but this, of course, is a map that has no statistical validity.

There is a great opportunity, as yet largely untapped, for the I.W. to add a major out of season tourist function as a Business and Conference Centre although if so further "wet weather" facilities would need to be provided.

Tourism supports roughly a quarter of all jobs in the Island in the high season but half of these disappear in the winter. It is important to recognise the *Multiplier Effect* in which both *direct* and *indirect* employment brings in revenue - not only to the hotels, shops, services etc. but, also, to the *Construction* industry, food suppliers etc. Also, the wages earned by those actually working inside the industry are often spent outside it. See also Appendix II and, particularly, Appendix IV.

TOURISM
Holiday Makers
Origin

Fig 51. Sketch Map to show results of random sample survey origin of 500 holiday makers - Sandown I.W.

(e) *Summary* - Undoubtedly, the I.W. is a popular Tourist regional centre, where the economic benefits of Tourism are self-evident. None-the-less it is prudent to end this section with a short survey, albeit limited and, largely, an element of *Economic Geography* -

SUMMARY SURVEY

PROS	CONS
• I.W. economy helped by many £Millions which is spread £Hundreds per head of population.	• There is a distinct social cost in providing full employment only during the peak season.
• Thousands of jobs would be lost without tourism.	• "All eggs in one basket" is not a sound base, economically.
• Land values increased by a tourist type development.	• Extra costs on local residents when public bodies have to provide extra amenities.
• Loss of tourism would mean Higher Local Government Taxes; reduced Services in I.W. and links with mainland.	• Increased congestion on roads, in car parks. More noise, litter etc.
• Withdrawal of many of the support services (e.g. Pubs, Cafés etc.)	• Overall higher costs in Public Services (e.g. Highways).
• Many "spin-off" facilities would not exist, to benefit residents.	• Loss of many visual amenities (e.g. sprawling campsites etc.)
• More jobs keep more Islanders on I.W.	• Inevitable accelerated rate of damage to environment, ecology.
	• Low rate of return on capital due to seasonality of demand.
	• More people create more hassle!

32. COMMUNICATIONS

(a) *Background* - In Geography "communications" does not mean the exchange of messages as you might think but, rather, the ways of getting about. Here, before looking at present day travel we first need to look back and to realise that only just over a century ago the chief method of getting about was either on foot or on horseback. Later, this was followed by travel by rail, road and then by air, whilst at sea you would have first sailed across to the I.W. and only later come by steam packet or paddle boat.

All of which effected the development of general communications in the Island as for example when, in section 17(5), you read of the arrival of the railway between Brading and Bembridge it is of interest to know that it was easier to bring most of the chalk for construction of the embankment from Portsdown Hill, on the mainland, by sea, rather than by horse and cart across the fields from the nearby Downs.

(b) **Rail** - It is hard to think of the train as the only means of transport for the whole Island. Yet, before the arrival of buses, cars and lorries that was the case. The first railway, from Cowes to Newport, opened in 1862 and was followed in 1864 by a service from Ryde (St. Johns) to Shanklin - and on to Ventnor in 1866. Other lines were added until, at one time, some 17 Companies operated over 55 miles of track (see Fig 52).

The Southern Railway took over all the Island's railways in 1923 until *nationalised* in 1948 when British Railways was formed: from 1952 onwards as more people by then were using the roads for travel, the railway lines were steadily closed.

Today, only 13.7 kms ($8^1/_2$ mls) of electric railway remains - between Ryde Pier Head and Shanklin - which service is invaluable in clearing large numbers of travellers quickly in the Summer, upon disembarking at Ryde. In addition the **"Isle of Wight Steam Railway"** operates from Wootton Station to Smallbrook, with its base at Havenstreet, for tourists.

Attempts have been made to open a Vectrail line between Newport and Cowes and, clearly, so long as the old tracks remain available, there is every opportunity of extending the use of rail with a trolley or rail bus or, better, as in modern urban development, an *L.R.T.* system (Light Rapid Transport), if only as an environmental measure to reduce pollution. This could well be in the form of a monorail system as, for example, in Sydney, Australia.

COMMUNICATIONS

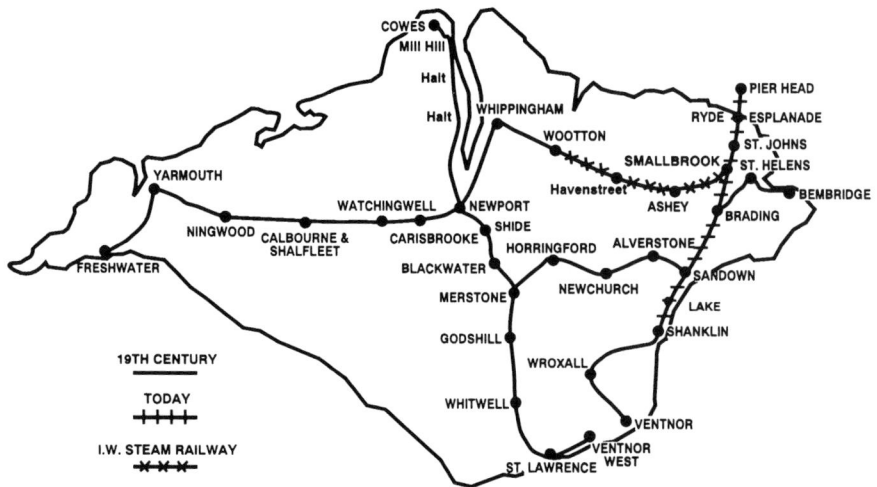

Fig 52. I.W. Rail Network

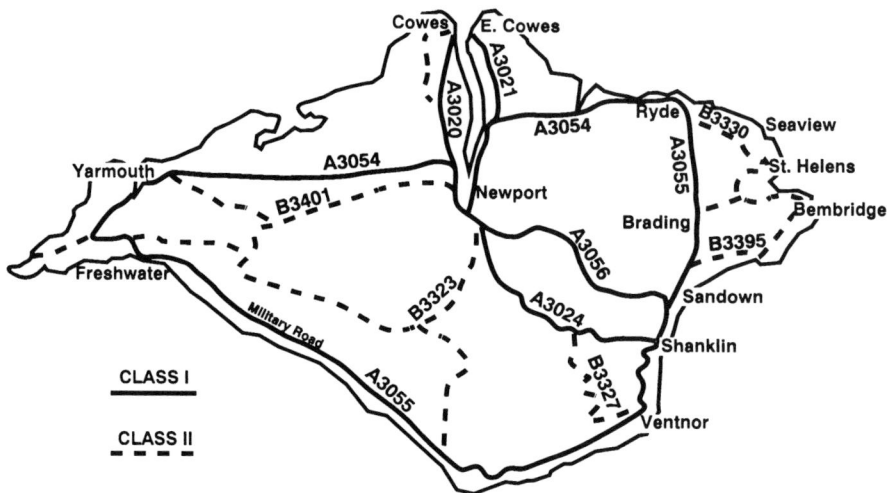

Fig 53. I.W. Road Network

(c) **Roads** - *Framework* - The first roads in the Island were developed from bridle paths (long before the present day large earth-moving equipment was invented) and the original routes of the *turnpikes* were much influenced by the hill formations. Look again at the Relief Map (Fig 12) and compare it with the pattern of roads in Fig 53.

As its name implies the A3055 Military Road was built by the Army, in about 1860, for quick passage by soldiers but, sadly, at its highest point under Compton Down this picturesque coastal road - used by around two million people each summer, faces an uncertain future due to the erosion of the cliff.

Road statistical details are given in Appendix II but suffice to note here that the road network of 787 kms (489 mls) has to sustain increasing traffic each year and ever heavier vehicle loads. In the Summer it is probably true to say that the Island road system carries the greatest number of vehicles per mile than in any other County.

A sample traffic flow is shown in Fig 54 over.

(d) **Bridges** - Currently, the longest bridge in the I.W. is at Brookgreen (O.S. 387835). The construction of a bridge across the River Medina has been mooted since 1890. If and whenever built such a fixed link between East and West Cowes would replace the existing *floating bridge* which hauls itself to and fro across the river on two 165 metre (540 feet) chains.

For many years there has been talk of constructing a bridge (or a tunnel) across the sea from the mainland to the Island. Apart from the huge economic problems involved such a scheme is unlikely to find favour with the majority of I.W. people since they treasure their status as an off-shore island race apart.

(e) **Footpaths and Bridleways** - The I.W. has a well-signed network of public rights of way and its total length of 830 kms (516 mls) is reckoned to be the most dense in the country.

Following the many *TRAILS* available is a most interesting activity.

(f) **Transport** - According to vehicle numbers it is reckoned that there are approximately 50,000 cars, 3,000 heavy goods and 10,000 other vehicles on the roads in the Island i.e 102 cars per 1.6km (mile) of road. Car ownership is marginally higher in the I.W. where, due to its dispersed population, it is widely used for travel to work from the rural areas; over one million cars cross the Solent each year, nearly 18,000 coaches and almost 20,000 commercial vehicles.

(g) **Sea** - One of the earliest records of a passenger service was in 1774 when "sailing packet boats left from Southampton every day, except Mondays" and when the weather was against them a journey of up to seven hours could be expected!

Today, there are six crossing routes to the I.W. (Fig 55). Something of the order of 8 million passengers (including I.W. residents) cross the sea each year using the ferries-cataramans, hydrofoils and hovercraft - which, incidentally, were invented in the I.W and have been in regular passenger service for over 30 years. Modern Roll-on/Roll-off (RoRo) ferries operate regular Winter crossings and, virtually, a shuttle service in the Summer to the terminals at Yarmouth, Cowes and Fishbourne.

Crossing times vary between 7 minutes by hovercraft from Ryde to Southsea; 35 minutes from Yarmouth to Lymington and 55 minutes from Cowes to Southampton by car ferry. See also Appendix II.

(h) **Air** - Airport facilities are available at the I.W. Airport at Sandown and flights are arranged from Bembridge Airport although Customs facilities have to be made in advance. The nearest mainland airports at Eastleigh (Southampton), 12 minutes away, and Hurn (Bournemouth) provide linking services but as yet, there are no scheduled regular air links to or from the I.W.: only Bembridge Airport has a concrete runway.

COMMUNICATIONS

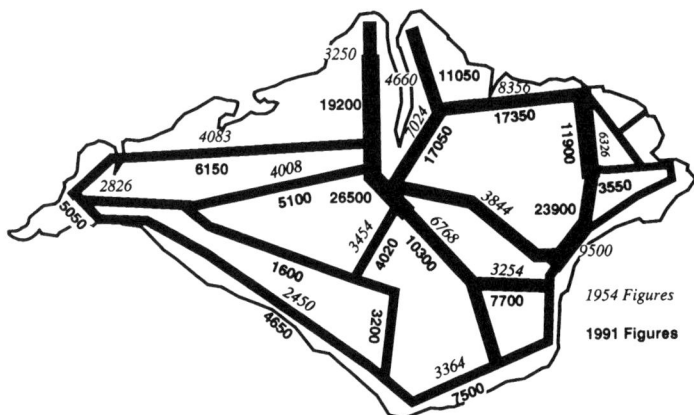

Fig 54. I.W. Traffic Flow - comparative figures

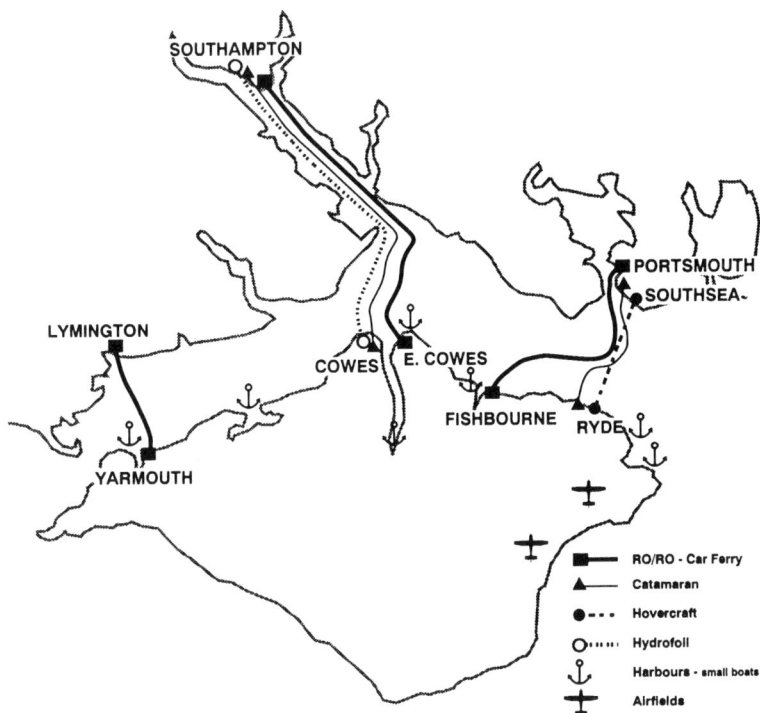

Fig 55. I.W. Links with the Mainland

33. POPULATION

The study of population and, in its wider context to include studies of *social science, ethnology* and *anthropology* - or what is known as **Demography** is fascinating in the extreme. Equally, on a small scale as for the I.W., these studies all help to measure and quantify the characteristics of the people, explain their past and foresee their future - except, that, it is the last phrase where the *statisticians* so often go so wrong!

(a) *Growth* - There are many elements in the analysis of a population of a place and only a very limited study in very general terms is possible in a book of this nature; for the more serious student some extra figures and references are given on page 108.

First, however, look at Fig 56 to see how the total population of the I.W. has grown over the last two centuries, compared with the rest of England and Wales. Roughly, in the 19th century, it grew by nearly four times and in the 20th by a further one and half times: overall from 22,000 to 126,000. Can we now estimate the total population in the first Census (2001) of the 21st Century? See also Appendix II.

(b) *Density* - Next, where do all the people in the I.W. live and do they always stay there? Many years ago the writer set up a model in school to test the theory that population movement in the I.W. was reflecting the national trend viz. a steady move from N-S and W-E. The answers to both questions and the model are in Fig 57. Based on the 1991 Census figures the present *Population Density* of the I.W. is:-

332.2 per sq.km or 860 per sq.mile

compared, roughly, to the U.K. density of 230 per 2.59 sq.km/mile. However, watch out on all statistics as it is also true to say that although the country of China contains over a quarter of the whole World's population its density is far less than that of the I.W.- for we also need to consider area size. Lastly, it is significant but quite understandable that the older, retired people live in the coastal areas whilst the younger and working people all tend to live nearer the centre of the Island - this is part of the data obtained from a Census.

POPULATION

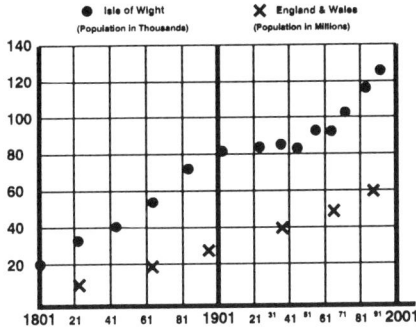

Fig 56. Population Growth

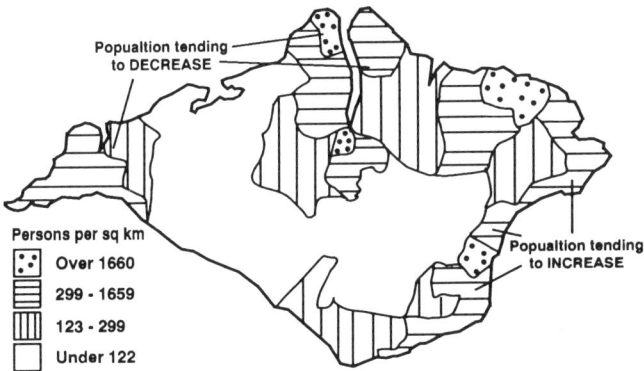

Fig 57. Population Density

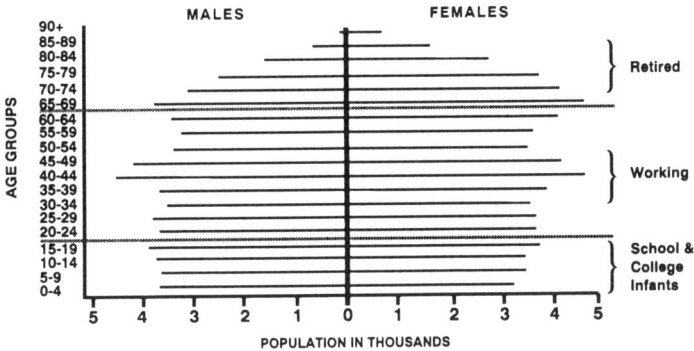

Fig 58. Age/Sex Graph

59

POPULATION

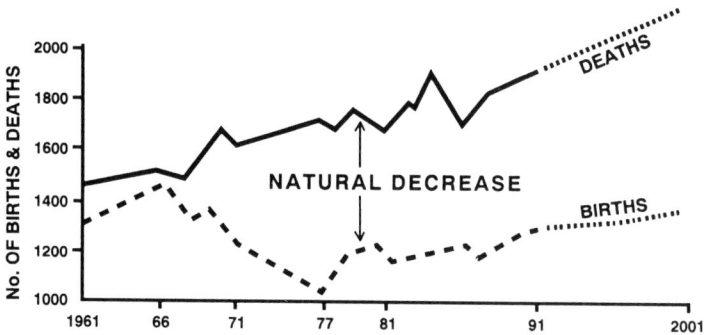

Fig 59. I.W. Birth & Deaths

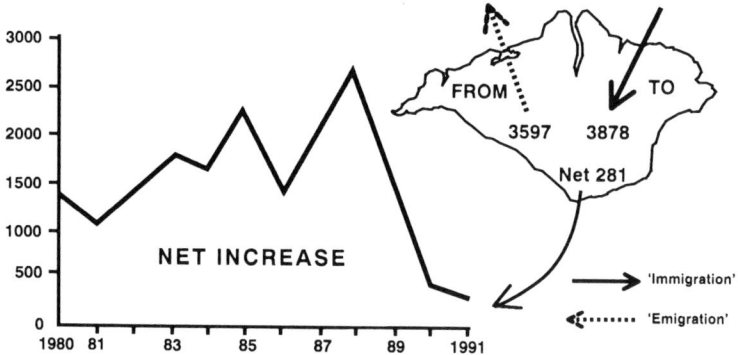

Fig 60. Migration

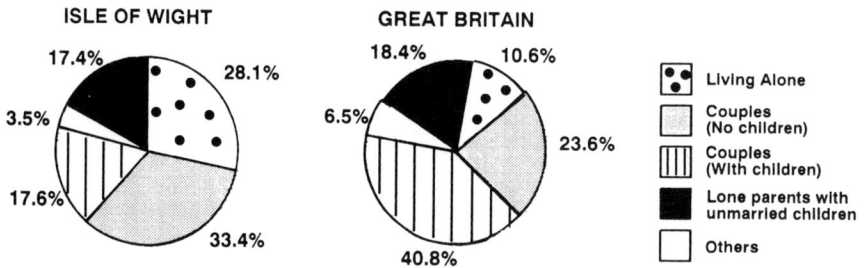

Fig 61. Households - comparision of composition with the rest of Britain

(c) *Age/Sex Graphs* - These are sometimes called "Population Pyramids". They are drawn in age and male/female groupings, as in Fig 58, together with the numbers involved in each five year division. From these pyramids, by examining the shape, Demographers are able to draw many conclusions. In this instance it is easy to see the imbalance between the proportions of retired, working and the young people. Clearly the I.W. has a top-heavy population of elderly people (where the females noticeably outlive the males). At the last Census this figure of 26.4% of the total population was the highest figure of any County in England and Wales and compared with an average U.K. figure of 18.3%.

In the next part, in order to investigate the problems of employment, housing and settlement in general we shall look at other items, under.

(d) *Births and Deaths* - These two factors have the most important effect on the levels of population. Study of Fig 59 shows that the *Birth Rate* in the I.W., although fairly consistent in the last decade, is tending to grow only very gradually, if at all. Meanwhile, the *Death rate* has been rising that much faster and now exceeds births by nearly 50%. Where the Death Rate exceeds the Birth Rate this is called the *Natural Decrease* and, it follows, vice versa, a *Natural Increase*.

In the I.W. there has been a steady decrease of population over the years - which trend is likely to continue - especially as children grow up and then leave the I.W in search of a job.

(e) *Ethnic Groups* - The I.W. has a very small non-white population of 0.73%, of whom half were born in the U.K., compared with the non-white ethnic group of 8.7% in the S.E. Region. See Appendix II for details.

(f) *Migration* - The third and a key factor in our enquiry into the Island's population statistics is Migration. Although, technically the terms *"immigration"* and *"emigration"* apply to movements of people between countries they are used in Fig 60 to demonstrate how this group, added to the resident population, represent a net increase in the overall total numbers.

Of course this does **not** include the many thousands of visiting holiday makers who swell our numbers each year.

In concluding this section, it remains to emphasise the geographical importance of using population statistics in order to examine the social, environmental and, above all, the economic future of the I.W. Those who make political judgments would be wise to follow suit!

34. HOUSING

In this section let us first look at the people and the nature of their different homes - see Fig 61 and note the Key. Comparing the I.W. with the rest of Great Britain we can immediately see that there is a much higher number of people living alone in the Island and proportionately fewer "traditional" families (comprising two adults and two children). Of interest the Census statistics (not shown in the pie graph) also confirm the significantly higher number of I.W. mothers, under twenty years of age, than in the rest of England and Wales.

Before leaving this subject we now take a brief look at the types of *households* in which the Islanders live - which is also part of the studies in *Urban Geography* and is referred later under *"Settlement"*. It is true to say that data about the houses and their location can be of great value in any geographical analysis (hence the Table on Dwellings, 1991 in the Appendix).

The majority of Island homes are *detached* - more so in the rural areas, *flats* are largely confined to the urban areas; about 80% of Island people own their homes (or, are buying them), including a number of *second homes* - particularly in the East Wight. The 1991 Census listed 51,239 households on the Island - an increase of 12.3% over the last ten years; the average household size is now 2.35 persons, per household and continues to fall. See also Appendix II.

35. EMPLOYMENT

(a) *Labour Force* - We have seen from the Age/Sex diagram (Fig 58) that the I.W. population structure shows a significant fall-off in the middle age ranges. If we select the 16 to 64 age groups which, in the Census 1991, numbered nearly 70,000 persons, we can then break this number down into those actually available for employment viz. 30,371

EMPLOYMENT

MEN

6616
399
3760
976
5785
18620

WOMEN

2258
266
1560
8369
11325
9432

- ☐ Unemployed
- ⊡ "Inactive"
- ■ Full Time
- ▨ Part Time
- ⦚ Self-employed
- ▦ Training

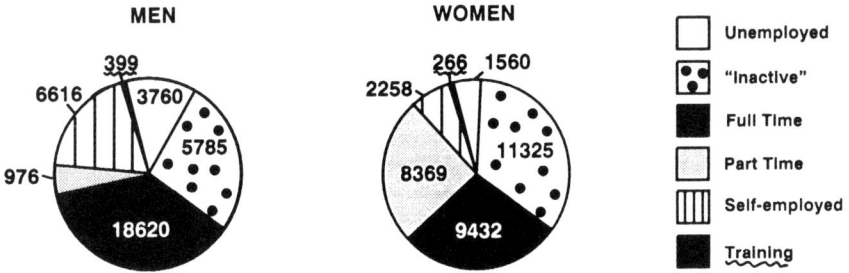

Fig 62. Labour Force - Breakdown

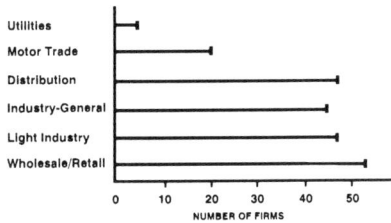

Utilities
Motor Trade
Distribution
Industry-General
Light Industry
Wholesale/Retail

0   10   20   30   40   50
NUMBER OF FIRMS

Fig 63. Company Types - Industrial Estates

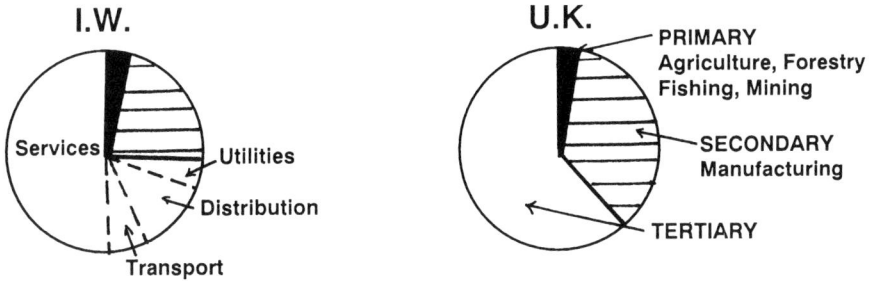

I.W.

Services
Utilities
Distribution
Transport

U.K.

PRIMARY
Agriculture, Forestry
Fishing, Mining

SECONDARY
Manufacturing

TERTIARY

Fig 64. Employment Structure - comparison only

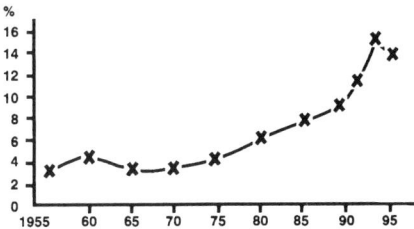

%
16
14
12
10
8
6
4
2
0
1955 60 65 70 75 80 85 90 95

Fig 65(a). Unemployment - Annual

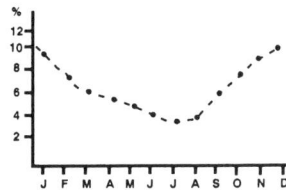

%
12
10
8
6
4
2
J F M A M J J A S O N D

Fig 65(b). Monthly - Trend

or 84% of the males and 21,887 or 66% of the females. The remainder being classed as "economically inactive" i.e. sick, disabled or not seeking work - for example, mothers, students. See Fig 62 and Appendix II.

(b) *Categories* - For analytical reasons, people's jobs are classified into "social classes". The I.W. percentage figures are as under:-

Professional (Doctors, Teachers, Lawyers etc)	6.0
Managerial and Technical (People in charge)	29.3
Skilled: non-manual (Qualified)	12.9
Skilled: manual (Highly trained)	26.2
Partly-skilled	16.9
Unskilled	5.3
Others	2.2

(c) *Commuters - trans Solent* - It is estimated that up to 700 professional, managerial and skilled persons travel daily/weekly to and from work on the mainland and just under 200 people travel to work in the I.W. from Lymington, Southampton and Portsmouth.

(d) *Industries - in general* - In the first half of the century large industries were based on Cowes, Newport and Ryde but, since then, there has been a steady fall in the number of big industries and, now, the majority of I.W. firms are small and employ less than ten workers.

This is exemplified in the *Industrial Estates* at Somerton, Ventnor, Gunville, Dodnor, Lake and Riverway where, in the main, the development has been *"trade"* rather than *"industry"*: the latter has largely been directed towards individual sites - for which adequate land is available. See Fig 63 for Company types.

The breakdown of the employment structure (see section 26) in the Island is given in Fig 64.

36. UNEMPLOYMENT

The number of unemployed persons on the Island continues to rise annually. However, the monthly changes vary dramatically due to the seasonal trends. A high proportion of people are only needed during the holiday season in the hotel, catering and tourist trades - some of whom come to the I.W. specially at this time. Sadly, it follows that the seaside towns thus tend to be the areas where most unemployment occurs in the Winter: this is all part of the Island's economic problems which will be looked at later in the book. The graphs in Fig 65 are self-evident.

37. SETTLEMENT

(a) *General* - High among the physical/human *relationships* that interest geographers is where people live and why? This idea of where people gather is called *settlement*. Those who live in towns are said to live in *urban* areas whilst the countryfolk live in *rural* areas.

The I.W. has no cities and, by comparison with the mainland, no large towns. It has three main types of settlement viz. small *Towns, Villages* and *Hamlets* (plus the occasional farm or *Homestead*), all of which vary in size, shape and the number of inhabitants - all for different reasons.

(b) *Early Settlers* - If, for example, we look back to the anglo-saxons, who came to the I.W. after the Romans left in 400 A.D., they were most likely to be *subsistence* farmers who needed shelter and water plus land to cultivate and to herd their animals. The chalklands were particularly attractive to them as they provided clean, dry sites with a high *water table*, flints for their tools and nearby forest for hunting deer, wild boar etc. Thus (as briefly referred in section 9 and Fig 10) early villages grew up on the line of springs, protected from the northerly winds, as in Fig 66 over. Before then, apart from their longbarrows and longstone there is little solid evidence of site habitation of earlier man still remaining in the I.W. The equable climate welcomed settlers, as it does today but, even by the time of the Domesday Book in 1086, only 88 place names were recorded with a total count of 1068 people.

Fig 67 identifies some of the earlier settlements in the I.W. but, owing to the difficulties of crossing the sea to the Island, it was much

SETTLEMENT

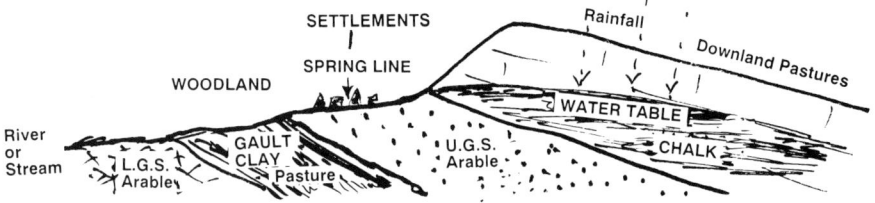

Fig 66. Early 'Spring-Line' Settlement

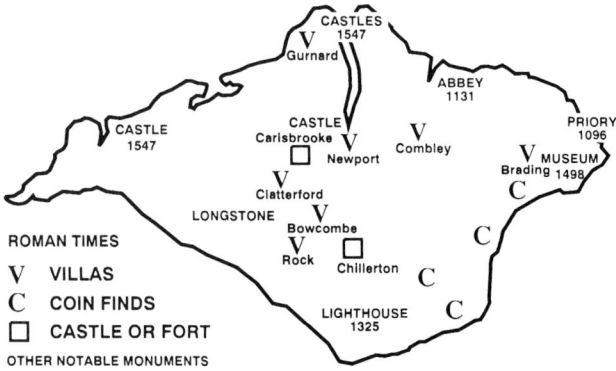

Fig 67. Early Settlements in the I.W.

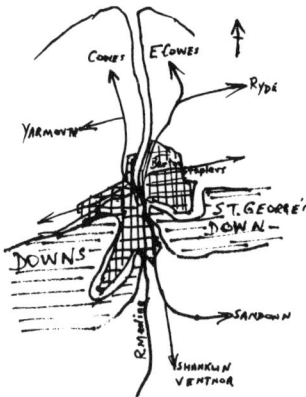

Fig 68. Sketch Map to show the position of Newport

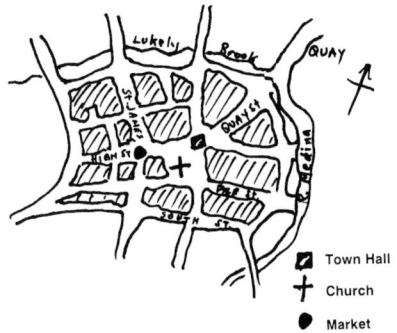

Fig 69. Sketch - Newport - early 17th century

later before the population numbers began to rise and settlements began to form at key points. Among the earliest towns being **Newport** at the crossroads of the I.W. (Figs 68 & 69).

(c) *Sites and Location* - *physical* - There are many factors involved in determining the position of town settlements: taking **Newport** as an example it has grown up where it is, because:-

- It is in the centre of the I.W. at a major route crossing point i.e. centre of communications.
- It is conveniently located in the gap of the central ridge of the chalk downs i.e. a "Gap" town.
- It is at the head of the river valley and at the "lowest bridging point" of the River Medina.
- It has a sheltered harbour and docks on a tidal estuary.
- It is near to a good defensive site.

(d) *Function* - *human* - All settlements have a different part to play and each one performs a variety of *functions*: in the case of **Newport**:-

- It became the chief *Market town* and inland *Port.*
- It is the *Capital town.*
- It is the *Administrative* and *Commercial* centre.
- It is an important centre for *Shopping* and *Services* - e.g. Fire, Police, Energy, Hospital, Library etc., etc.

All settlements are living units, reflecting their own character and personality. Contrasting with **Newport**, **Cowes** grew up as a *Ferry port, Industrial centre, Holiday Resort* and remains an international and world famous *Yachting centre* whereas in the case of **Sandown/Shanklin** their good beaches, attractive scenery, "sunshine record", pier, theatres, zoo, water and other sports etc. all mark them, clearly, as *Tourist* and *Holiday centres.*

(e) *Shape of settlements* - Unless deliberately planned as a settlement and, then, usually in a regular shape, villages and towns steadily grow into a pattern (Fig 70) - examples in the I.W. are:-

Dispersed	- scattered or isolated	e.g. **Billingham Manor**
Linear	- along a river or a road	e.g. **Arreton**
Round	- surrounding a green	e.g. **St. Helens**
Concentric	- outwards from a core	e.g. **Newport**

(f) *Architecture and Buildings* - Most of the main period styles of architecture are to be found in the Island. Initially the stone was quarried and the bricks were made in the Island but the materials have now been almost all worked out. Artificial stone blocks feature in new developments.

The study of buildings provides a real clue to both the age and growth of settlements. There is no better way to investigate an area than by looking at the different types of houses, checking their historical sequence and mapping out the growth, starting as in Fig 69 with the church or inn. There are over thirty villages in the I.W. and a sample study extract is given later. (Note: It is better to look at a small part in detail than attempt total cover).

In the Island as a whole, some interesting building developments include:- Tudor/Jacobean Manor Houses, grouped with farm, church etc. as at **Yaverland, Mottistone** and **Arreton.**
Early stone/thatched cottages - **Brighstone, Shorwell**
Water mills - **Calbourne, Alverstone**
Regency - early Victorian housing at **Ryde**

Travelling from **Downend** (O.S. 532876) via **Staplers** and **Barton** towards the town centre of **Newport** locate the style and type of housing in sequence i.e. bungalows, detached houses, semi-detached, housing estate, flats, terraced houses - towards the Bus Station and superstores. Now, read on and relate the foregoing to the zonal structure of towns as in Fig 71 opposite and in (g) over.

68

SETTLEMENT

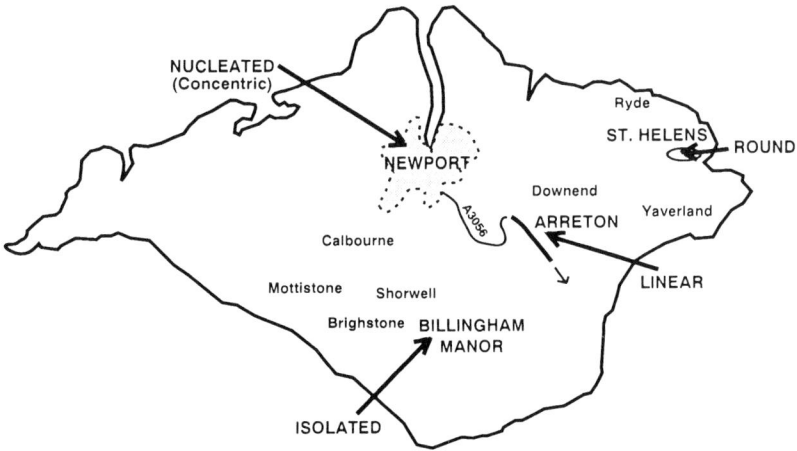

Fig 70. Types & shapes of Settlements & Building Developments

CONCENTRIC MODEL

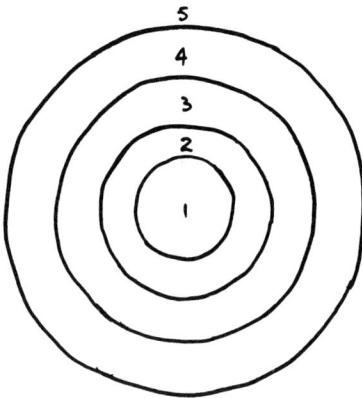

SECTOR MODEL
(Allows different pattern to accommodate lines of communication, physical barriers etc.)

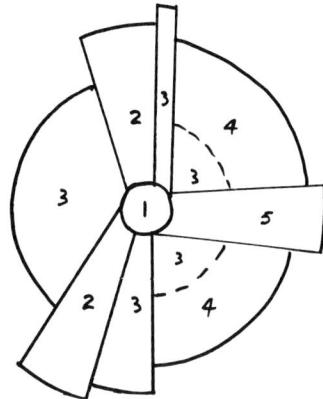

1. CENTRAL AREA - Shops, offices & C.B.D.
2. MIDDLE ZONE - Old Residential, now offices & flats
3. MIDDLE ZONE - Lower class residential
4. OUTER ZONE - Medium class residential
5. URBAN FRINGE - High class residential

Fig 71. Urban Structure - Zones (after Burgess & Hoyt)

(g) *Structure of Towns* - **ZONES** - The structural pattern of towns has been categorised into many different model types. To retain the simple approach, we suggest a basic division of four zones, again using Newport as our example:-

(i) **Central or Nuclear area** - the oldest part of a town, centred about its origin, mostly non-residential, containing the *Central Business District* (C.B.D.), often wholly or partly *rejuvenated* (i.e. in the case of Newport, the original central area demolished and replaced by the Bus Station, new shops and superstores).

(ii) **Middle Zone** - surrounding the core, of late 19th early 20th century buildings, some terraced housing - partly decaying but now with clearance and rebuilding.

(iii) **Outer Zone** - built up after World War I, move towards industrial development, housing estates and away from terraced houses.

(iv) **Urban Fringe** - moving further outwards through higher class housing, detached bungalows all mostly after World War II.

Perhaps the foregoing is too greatly oversimplified for the purist geographer but, hopefully, it will help to relate with the models in Fig 71 and the studies to follow.

(h) *Urban Study - RYDE* - Various models have been suggested to demonstrate *Urban Structure*. Using the Sector Model the present day functions of the town are shown in Fig 72. Commercial development is discussed in section 38, following. It is of interest to note the effect that the sea and coastline have on the development pattern.

Ryde began as a straggling fishing village and, by mid 18th century, had grown into two *hamlets* - Upper Ryde (on the brow of the hill) and Lower Ryde at the bottom. It was constituted as a *town* in 1854 and received the Royal Charter in 1868. (Population then about 10,000). As a *Borough* it operated its own fire, water, police, magistrates and education services. Population 1991 was 25,811 (12,067 m/13,744 f).

The end of the Victorian and Edwardian eras and the loss of Royalty in the Island saw the departure of the large households which initially characterised Ryde pre World War I. Most have now been turned into holiday flats.

SETTLEMENT

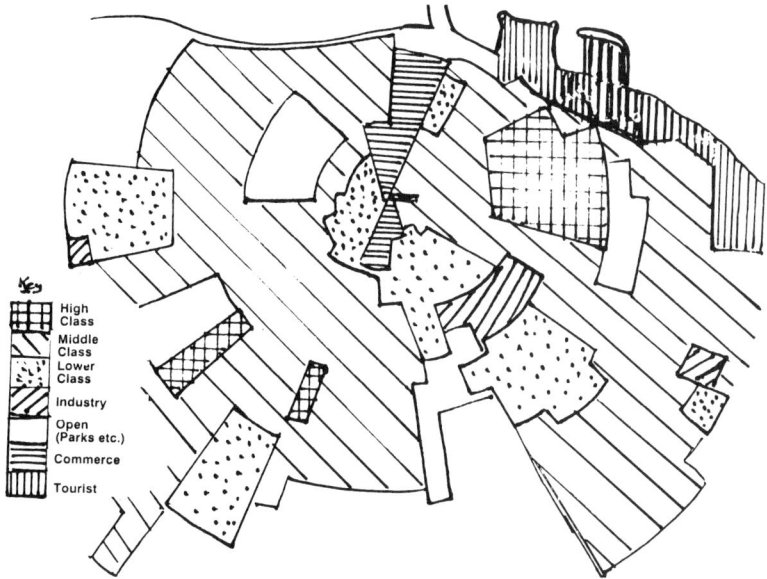

Fig 72. RYDE - Urban Study (after Doe)

Legend:
- High Class
- Middle Class
- Lower Class
- Industry
- Open (Parks etc.)
- Commerce
- Tourist

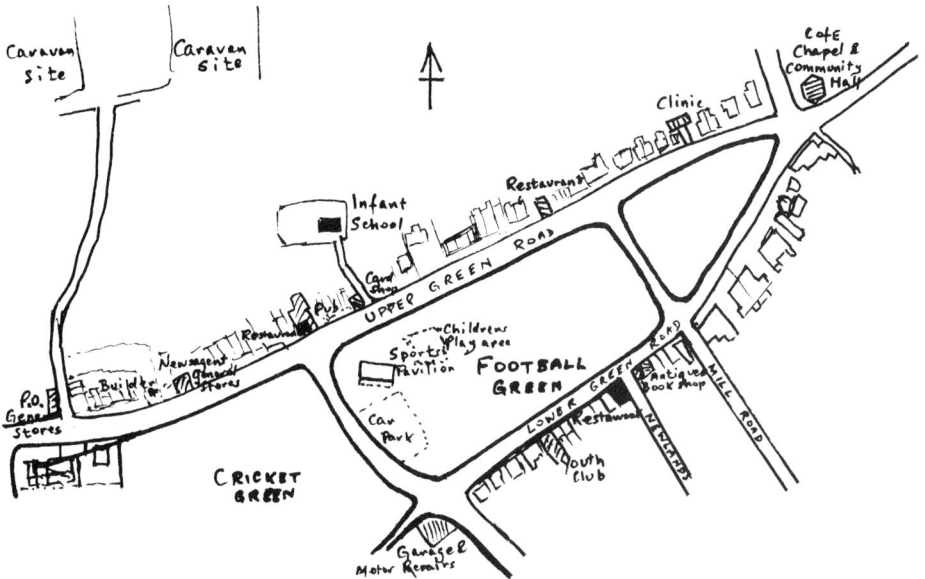

Fig 73. ST. HELENS Village Study - Field Sketch Map (see also Fig 76)

Before the pier was constructed in 1813, visitors were carried ashore from boats hauled up on the large adjacent sand banks. Today, visitors arrive in modern cataramans and hovercraft! Apart from its functions as a ferry arrival port and shopping centre, its main industry is now concentrated on tourism and it has steadily advanced as a holiday resort, although it still retains an element of light manufacturing activity.

(i) *Village Study - ST. HELENS* - Population 1,189 (558 m/631 f).

By complete contrast this small part of a village study is included since, not only has the I.W. over thirty villages and hamlets to investigate but, being typical of life in Britain 150 years ago, it is still an essential part of our history.

A study of this nature can also demonstrate, geographically, how the role of a village has changed and how this change can reflect social change in general. In the case of St. Helens, for example, count the total number of shops of each type in Fig 73 and match this finding with the following statistics, taken in March 1962:-

Food shops	10	Churches	3	Schools	1
Non Food shops	7	Halls	2	Pubs	2
Post Office	1	Garages	1	Surgeries	4
Buses (day)	60	Cafés	0	Clinics	1

See also Fig 76.

The principal feature of **St. Helens** is its Village Green, surrounded by a striking variety of different dwellings - including the notorious home of the smuggler's "Queen of Chantilly". A short distance north to the church (1717) which replaced the more ancient church, built in the 12th century by the Cluniac monks, now a *sea-mark*. The "Holystones" from its ruins were taken and used for scrubbing decks by Nelson's sailors.

The old flour mill, now demolished, at the harbour's edge where vessels used to bring cargoes to and from the mainland, the former railway sidings, gas holder and further afield on the "Duver", the golf links all testify to a by-gone age. Yet, where wooden boats were built you can now find hovercraft. Meanwhile the harbour, filled with sailing craft, continues to silt up, longshore drift persists and the off-shore spit grows ever closer as it attempts to close the harbour mouth. Add to this

the *Biogeography*, Environmental problems, gathering data, asking questions locally, classifying, checking with *secondary sources* making hypotheses and analysing the whole - and who says that a Village Study can't be great fun for student and holiday-maker alike?

38. SHOPPING
Retail and Service outlets

(a) *Mediaeval Times* - In the Middle Ages *markets* were to be found in **Newtown** and **Newport**, which grew up along the route between the River Medina and **Carisbrooke** castle. In those days, what are now St. Thomas' and St. James' Squares were then occupied by the Beast Market, the Butter Market, the Cheese Cross, the Corn Market and the Shambles (butchers stalls).

(b) *Yesteryear* - **Ryde** developed as a shopping centre, as with **Newport**, at the end of the 18th century; other smaller centres came into being later on at **Cowes, Sandown, Shanklin, Ventnor, Yarmouth** and **Freshwater**, located on Fig 74 over.

(c) *Retailing* - Over the past twenty years or so, the study of retailing and service industries has come to form another of the main themes in Human Geography. Its origins are traceable to a German Geographer called Christaller who developed a model called the "Central Place" theory. This was based on the size, spacing and functions of settlements and their effect on what, loosely, we call shopping.

Oversimplified, as in Fig 75 over, in the case of the I.W., it suggested that for small, everyday items you shopped in the local village, for a larger range and better choice you went to Newport or Ryde but if you wanted to buy such as a grand piano you probably travelled to Portsmouth or Southampton.

Look, now, at Fig 76 over, and note the changes in village shopping. Look at Union Street in Ryde, as an example of what is happening in the towns - where more and more shops are closing as out-of-town superstores are opening. All of these changes mainly due to the motor car where, in the Island, the growth of car ownership has been greater than most of Britain. This has led, as on the mainland, to carborne

SHOPPING

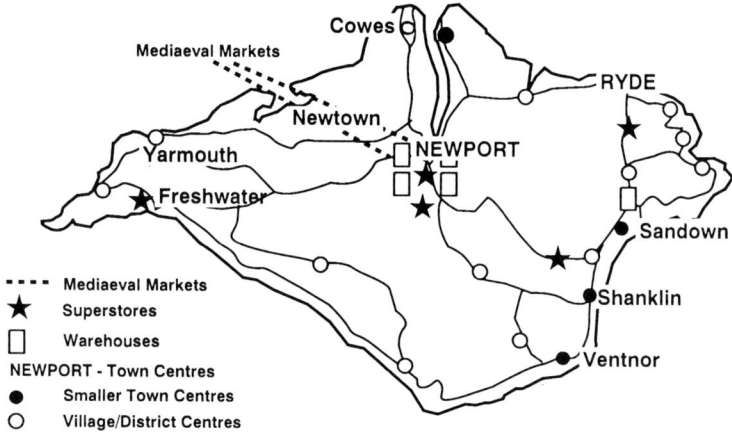

Fig 74. I.W. Shopping Centres

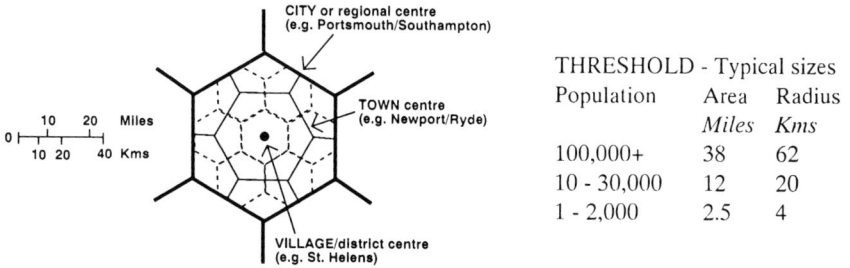

THRESHOLD - Typical sizes		
Population	Area	Radius
	Miles	Kms
100,000+	38	62
10 - 30,000	12	20
1 - 2,000	2.5	4

Fig 75. "Central Places" (model pattern (adapted) - after Christaller)

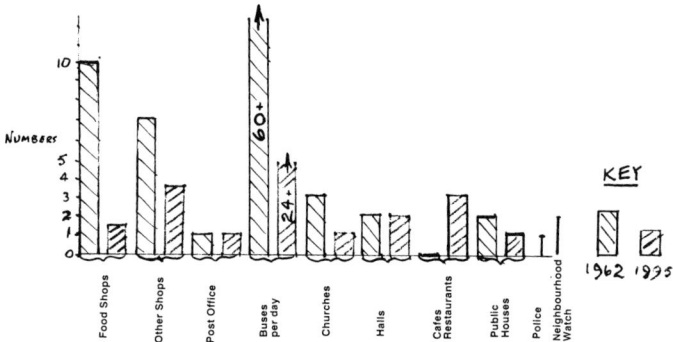

Fig 76. St. Helens Village - Graph to show the changes in some Retail & Services Outlets (see also Fig 73)

shoppers having a noticeable influence on the growth of retail warehousing and the larger multiple stores, aided by better choice, improved shopping technology and, because of the refrigerator at home, the advantages of buying in bulk - plus easy car parking. In consequence the quality of shopping life has improved for most people (particularly the many elderly folk in the I.W. - for whom some stores provide free bus travel).

(d) *Tomorrow* - What follows tomorrow is reflected in the village study that shows how the old order changeth (e.g. as in Fig 76) and is being replaced by a new way of life. Today, apart from the late night "convenience shop on the corner" in the rural areas and in spite of traffic quiet streets and environmental improvement schemes in the towns, there is a growing danger of urban decay in the town centres: at the moment the place of retail shops is being taken by non-retail outlets (e.g. offices, banks etc.) and "Take-aways". In the seaside towns even the number of gift shops for the tourists is declining in places.

So, in the I.W. the trend towards the out-of-town and larger retail units in either the Trading Estates or special, all-weather sites is still possible although, thankfully, much of our development continues in more central positions in both Newport and Ryde, competing with the growing *mail order* and future shopping from home, by computer, that is to come.

As a tourist region, the Island is fortunate in that "shopping" is becoming an increasing attraction to many holiday-makers, thereby adding to the Island's economic growth.

39. POLITICAL

(a) *Political Geography* - the field of study where politics and geography overlap and mutually influence each other. The I.W., for example, as an island, provides a measure of isolation and security. It is an obvious geographical element in its own right: the effects of its severance by the sea and its spatial extent are examined later.

(b) Formerly part of Southampton, the I.W. was constituted on 1st April 1890, as a separate **COUNTY**. Since then, the organisation of its *Local Authorities* has passed through a cycle of change - from Municipal and District Boroughs, Urban Districts, Rural Districts and Parishes to its present and, hopefully - exactly 105 years later, its final structure, whereby the Island is divided into 48 **Ward Divisions** which combine to form the **ISLE OF WIGHT COUNCIL**. The former and present boundary structures are shown in Figs 77 and 78 opposite.

(c) Today, the Island's political organisation is centred in **Newport** which received its first *Charter* in the reign of King Henry II. At national level the I.W. is represented by *one* **Member of Parliament** although the most ancient borough of **Newtown**, granted its Charter in 1256, previously represented the Island with *two* M.P.s until 1832.

(d) In view of its size and cohesion the Island is clearly best served by one unitary authority which is charged to retain the vital principle of control and the self-determination of their own public affairs by Island people. This it does with the exception of the Police, Probation and Health services. Its operational structure is outlined in section 40 over; its Logo and *Coat of Arms* are shown in Fig 80. The Heraldic description of the latter is given, under:-

> "The insular character of the County is represented by the Island lapped by conventional waves of the sea upon which the remainder of the achievement is based. Carisbrooke Castle and the Royal links are suggested by the Castle on the Shield. The supporters of the Shield in the forms of a horse and a sea horse, symbolise Agriculture and the Sea which have supported and conditioned the Island. The sea is further symbolised by the blue or 'azure' of the Shield and by

POLITICAL

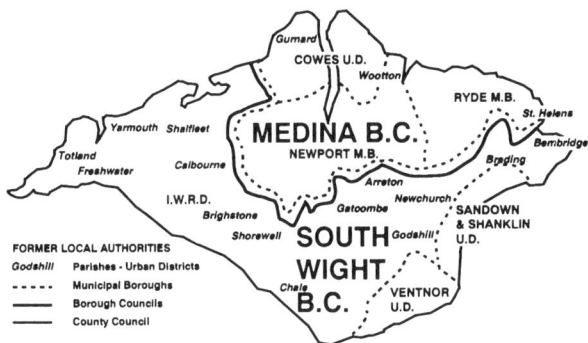

Fig 77. I.W. - Former Local Authorities - until May 1995

Fig 78. I.W. Council - Ward Divisions - from May 1995

1 Arreton & Newchurch
2 Ashey
3 Bembridge
4 Bembridge
5 Binstead
6 Brading
7 Brighstone & Shorwell
8 Calbourne, Shalfleet & Yarmouth
9 Carisbrooke East
10 Carisbrooke West
11 Chale, Niton & Whitwell
12 Cowes Castle 1
13 Cowes Castle 2
14 Cowes Central
15 Cowes Medina
16 East Cowes1
17 East Cowes 2

18 Fairlee
19 Freshwater, Afton
20 Freshwater, Norton
21 Gatcome, Godshill & Rookley
22 Gurnard
23 Lake 1
24 Lake 2
25 Mount Joy
26 Newport Central
27 Northwood
28 Osborne
29 Pan
30 Parkhurst
31 Ryde N.E.
32 Ryde N.W.
33 Ryde S.E.

34 Ryde S.W.
35 St. Helens
36 St. Johns 1
37 St. Johns 2
38 Sandown 1
39 Sandown 2
40 Seaview & Nettlestone
41 Shanklin Central
42 Shanklin North
43 Shanklin South
44 Totland
45 Ventnor 1
46 Ventnor 2
47 Wootton
48 Wroxall

Fig 79. Electoral Divisions

the anchors. Surmounting the helmet will be seen the 'mural crown', an embattled wall in the semblance of a crown."

(e) *Royalty* - The I.W was incorporated into the English realm in the reign of Edward I and although titular Lords of the Island were appointed until 1495 this title was changed to Captain for nearly 100 years when the title Governor came into use.

Robert Hammond, Governor, related to Cromwell, was in office at the time King Charles I was detained in Carisbrooke Castle - a notable incident in the history of the I.W. as was the burial of his daughter, Elizabeth, in St. Thomas' Church, Newport.

After a succession of Governors and nearly 200 years later Queen Victoria came to live at Osborne in 1861 and stayed there until she died in 1901. Her son-in-law Prince Henry of Battenburg was succeeded as Governor by his wife, Princess Beatrice until she died in 1944. Lord Mountbatten was appointed after the Seventh Duke of Wellington resigned and, in 1965, received his Letters Patent from Queen Elizabeth II in person at Carisbrooke Castle. His other title of Lord Lieutenant was added in 1974. He died, untimely, in 1979, since when the post of Governor has remained vacant, although the post of Lord Lieutenant still remains and carries responsibility for the magistracy, as the representative of H.M. the Queen, who also appoints the High Sheriff.

The Royal Yacht Squadron, occupying the site of King Henry VIII's West Cowes fort, has entertained our own and foreign royalty since the days of King George IV.

40. GOVERNMENT

If ever a title was invented to frighten off the would-be interested student - this is it! Yet, to the Human Geographer, this subject is an essential part of the Island's story - we need to know "Who does what and where?" on our behalf. In the I.W. the expression "Government" applies in two main areas - see over.

"A GEOGRAPHER'S LOOK AT THE I. W."

The following, missed at publication, should be inserted after "in 1979," in place of the last four lines, penultimate para 39(c), on page 78:-

"The separate post of Governor remained vacant until the appointment of Lord Mottistone C.B.E., now retired. His successor continues as the Lord Lieutenant - as the representative of H.M. the Queen, who also appoints the High Sheriff.

Currently, there is no Governor of the I.W. although it is the Author's opinion that H.R.H., The Princess Royal would be a very popular choice."

POLITICAL

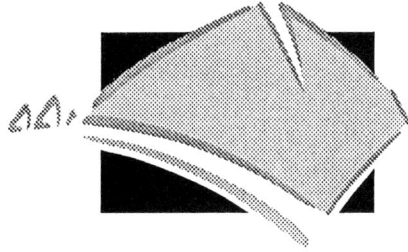

Fig 80. Coat of Arms and I.W. Council Logo

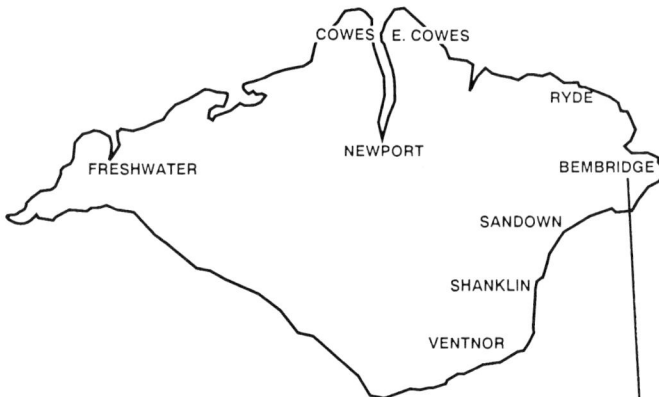

Fig 81. Community Information Points (C.I.P.s)

- Freephone & Fax facilities
- Community N. Bds.
- Local Information
- Displays, Exhibitions
- Leaflets, Forms
- Wightfax Service
- Trained Staff

Fig 82. Typical C.I.P. (Bembridge Library)

(a) *Central Government* - Which maintains a number of Departmental agencies viz.:-

In Newport

Dept. of SOCIAL SECURITY -	which deals with over 25% of I.W. people concerning "Benefit" assistance.
Dept. of INLAND REVENUE -	dealing with all I.W. Tax matters and records.
CROWN PROSECUTION SERVICE (Home Office)	- liaising with Police Force.
H.M. PRISON SERVICE	- overall responsibility for the operational running of the three I.W. Prisons.

In Cowes

H.M. CUSTOMS & EXCISE - (Dept. Inland Revenue)	oversees the arrival of all foreign vessels and aircraft, small boat Island sailors and private aircraft from abroad.

(b) *Local Government*

(i) *The I.W. Council* is an assembly of 48 elected councillors, each drawn from an *Electoral Ward Division* - Figs 78 & 79.

This *Unitary Authority* - the first in the country, began in May 1995, provides an all-Island service paid for both by central government grant and taxes raised locally. The day-to-day running of the Island's affairs is managed by a system of Directorates, responsible as follows:-

TITLE	SERVICE
Cultural & Leisure	- Arts, Libraries, Museums, Sporting and Leisure functions.
Engineering & Technical	- Roads, Traffic, Car Parks, Cemeteries, Transport, Waste, Coastal engineering.
Community & Social	- Housing and Social care.
Finance	- Council Tax, Benefits (Housing), all Accounting, Information Technology.

TITLE	SERVICE
Public Protection	- Fire, Rescue, Emergency planning, Trading, Environmental Health.
Economic & Tourism	- Economic development, Marketing and Promotion of Tourism.
Education	- Schools, Youth Service and support services.
Environmental & Planning	- Planning, Building control and Countryside Management.
Legal & Administration	- Legal & Admin, Registrar, C.I.Ps.
Corporate Services	- Public Relations, Civic Affairs.

(ii) *Community Information Points* (C.I.Ps) operate at each of the places in Fig 81 and are linked direct to the above.

(iii) *Parish/Town Councils* throughout the Island look after the immediate local community affairs.

(c) *Summary*

Thus, we see that the I.W. people are "governed" at three levels:-

1. By Central Government (or Parliament) from London but with a presence in the I.W., as in (a) above.

2. By the I.W. Council from Newport, which provides all our many services as outlined in (b) above.

3. With our local Town/Parish Councils acting consultatively.

41. SOCIAL GEOGRAPHY

Social Geography incorporates the humane study of society and its community organisations: some of these, applicable to the I.W., include:-

(a) *Education* - In the I.W., education is based on comprehensive, co-educational schools - operated on a three-tier system - Primary (5-9yrs), Middle (9-13yrs) and High (13-16/18yrs), located as in Fig 83. Of these, some 25 Primary and/or Middle Schools are under the aegis of C of E or R.C churches. There are also 2 Special Schools providing for those with learning difficulties. See also Appendix II.

SOCIAL

SCHOOLS
(Census 1991)

●	46	Primary
△	16	Middle
■	5	High
○	4	Independent
✕	1	F.E. College
·	74	Playgroups
S	2	Special
Y	12	Youth Clubs
L	11	Libraries

PUPILS

●	6,867
△	5,320
■	4,874
○	1,239

Fig 83. I.W. Education

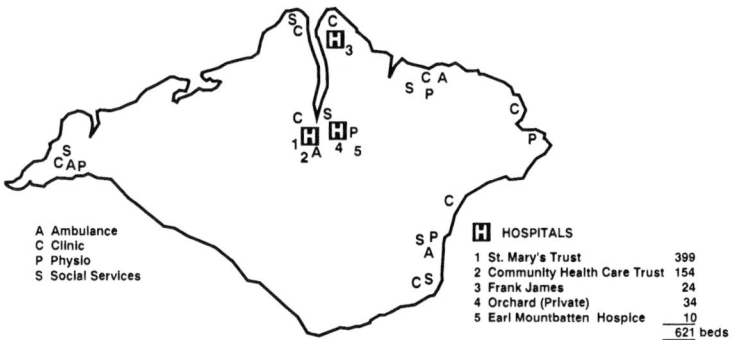

A Ambulance
C Clinic
P Physio
S Social Services

H HOSPITALS

1	St. Mary's Trust	399
2	Community Health Care Trust	154
3	Frank James	24
4	Orchard (Private)	34
5	Earl Mountbatten Hospice	10
		621 beds

Fig 84. I.W. Health & Social Services, 1995

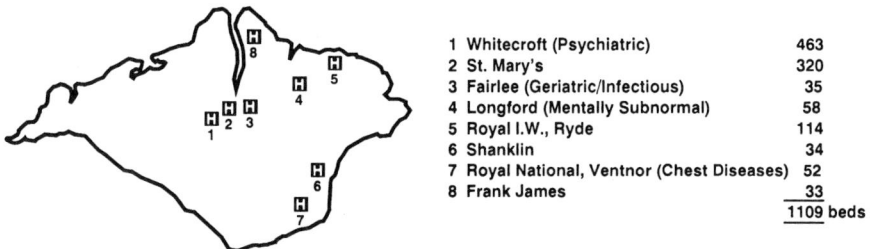

1	Whitecroft (Psychiatric)	463
2	St. Mary's	320
3	Fairlee (Geriatric/Infectious)	35
4	Longford (Mentally Subnormal)	58
5	Royal I.W., Ryde	114
6	Shanklin	34
7	Royal National, Ventnor (Chest Diseases)	52
8	Frank James	33
		1109 beds

Fig 85. I.W. Hospital Services, 1962

82

In addition there are 4 Independent Schools and the I.W. College of Arts & Technology which provides a wide choice of nearly 200 Further Education and Vocational courses. Apart from the Open University there are no Higher Educational facilities on the Island - with the result that the more academic students have to cross to the mainland to study at University level and, thence, to pursue careers beyond the Solent.

An Island-wide number of Youth Clubs, Libraries and Museum services are operated by the I.W. Council which also supports the independent Arts Centre on Newport Quay.

Look again at Fig 12 and see how the physical geography impinges on human activities and their distribution in the Island.

(b) *Health* - In general terms, Health Service funding in the I.W. comes largely from Central Government via the Wessex Regional Authority to various Island bodies in order to provide, together with the I.W. Council, the numerous health, social and community services available. Fig 84 shows the location of the health establishments in the I.W. but not the G.P., Dental or Optical services.

The increasing inward migration of the elderly to the Island adds to the already over-stretched care requirements for the aged. It also helps to explain why the natural decrease in the I.W. population occurs, as is mentioned in section 33(d). Of interest, in the 1991 Census (Fig 59) the number of Live Births recorded (1,337) was exceeded by the number of Deaths (1,953), by nearly 50%; the main cause of death being heart disease, closely followed by cancer.

Reference back to Fig 53 and the Island's radial network of roads will demonstrate why the modern St. Mary's Hospital has been located in its present site. Here, the general, emergency and accident facilities for the whole Island are readily available to all within a maximum distance of 19 kms (12 miles). NOTE also, the advance in medical science and changes in the hospital services over the past thirty years - by reference to the map in Fig 85. See also Appendix II.

(c) *Social Services* - A very wide range of social services is operated by the I.W. Council from Newport - with a network of outlying neighbourhood offices as in Fig 84. The principal services include those for the elderly and home cover, the mentally ill and handicapped, child care and, particularly, a number of therapeutic services for those with learning problems and the disabled.

Happily, there is a growing awareness and provision in the whole of the Island - at all levels - for those in wheel chairs. (See the detailed "Guide to the I.W. for the Disabled Person")

(d) **I.W.C.P.** - Because it clearly serves a positive community need, mention is made under this heading of the local newspaper, the "I.W. County Press", published weekly since 1884, with a circulation today that reaches almost every household in the Island.

42. EMERGENCY SERVICES

(a) *Police* - There is no doubt that matters of law & order and crime and its prevention are high on the list of social factors in any human geographic studies attempting to monitor "quality of life". Here in the I.W. not withstanding the existence of three prisons, a huge annual influx of visitors and a road system less than modern, we are more fortunate than our mainland contemporaries. For example, expressed in simple figures - the average crime rate in the U.K. is 99 per 1000 population compared with 66 per 1000 in the Island; whereas in Surrey policing costs approx. 35p per day, per person it only costs 23p (1994) in the I.W. where the main crime is burglary, centred on the urban areas.

The I.W. Police Force is part of the Hampshire Constabulary and operates as a Sub Division, based in Newport. It is thinly spread around a number of Principal Police Stations (see Fig 86) and it comprises regular officers in uniform, C.I.D., forensic and traffic officers, dog handlers and a small force of volunteer Special Constabulary officers. In addition a marine vessel, based at Cowes, patrols the Solent and I.W. coastline. Also, at present there are over 400 *Neighbourhood Watch* schemes liaising with the police.

(b) *Fire* - Responsibility for the Fire and Rescue services is with the I.W. Council. The Headquarters in Newport is supported by smaller units spaced around the Island (see Fig 86) to ensure that emergency calls are dealt with in accordance with National Standards laid down for

SOCIAL (& COMMUNITY)

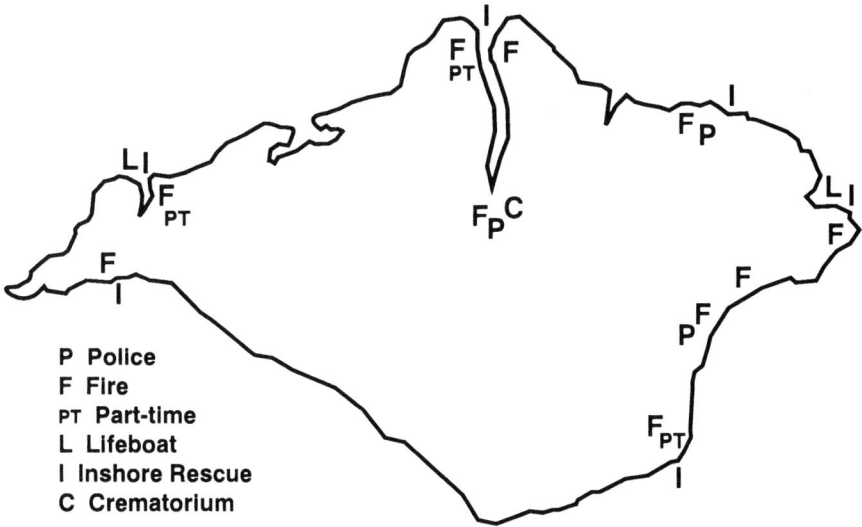

P   Police
F   Fire
PT Part-time
L   Lifeboat
I   Inshore Rescue
C   Crematorium

Fig 86. I.W. Emergency Services (& Crematorium)

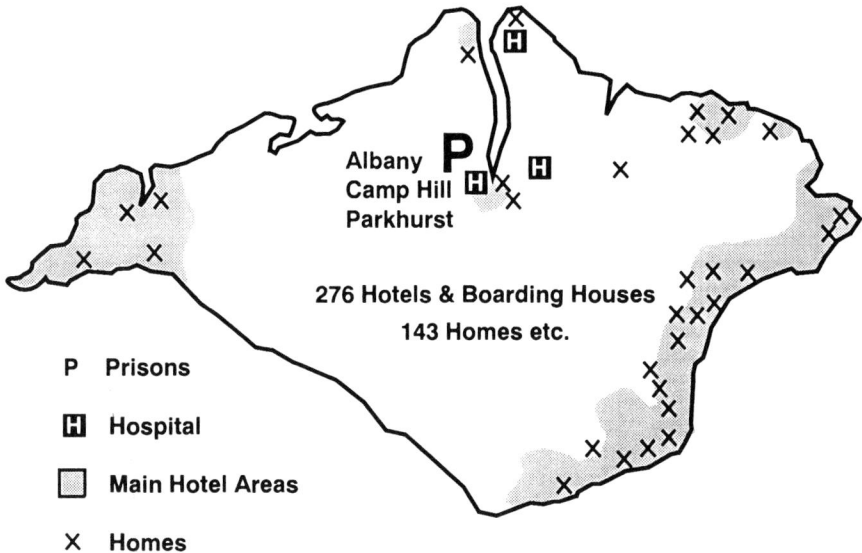

Albany
Camp Hill
Parkhurst

276 Hotels & Boarding Houses
143 Homes etc.

P   Prisons

H   Hospital

☐   Main Hotel Areas

X   Homes

Fig 87. I.W. Communal Establishments

quick turnouts. The Fire Brigade comprises a core of full-time officers and fire-fighters, backed up by a larger number of retained part-time personnel. Lesser realised but equally important functions of the Brigade's responsibilities include rescue, salvage, fire prevention, chemical incident and Inspection services for which are issued Certificates to factories, hotels, shops etc.

(c) *Sea* - The Coastguard maintains watch from stations at Bembridge, Ventnor and the Needles, with one full-time Sector Officer and a number of part time officers. The total Marine Rescue Services are controlled from the Marine Centre at Lee-on-Solent, co-ordinating with the R.N. and R.A.F.

In the I.W. there are two large all-weather R.N.L.I. deep sea vessels (at Bembridge and Yarmouth), one inshore life-boat at Bembridge, supported by voluntary rescue services at Cowes, Ryde and Freshwater. In 1991, there was a total of 89 launches, spending 177 hours at sea and saving 48 lives as well as property worth £1,355,500.

The R.N.L.I. Training Centre at East Cowes also builds inshore inflatable lifeboats.

43. COMMUNITY

Communal Establishments - The disposition of the various communal establishments in the I.W. is shown in Fig 87. This sketch map, based on the Census returns, helps to identify where - largely due to their age - residents live in medical and care establishments, children are looked after in homes and large numbers of visitors stay in hotels and guest houses. Not surprisingly, apart from the inmates in prison and patients in hospital, most of these are concentrated along the coast, mainly on the South East.

Social Geographers will be interested to note that in the I.W. Census figures, no one was recorded as "living rough on the Island"- perhaps another factor in considering our quality of life!

44. UTILITY SERVICES
(a) *WATER*

(i) *The National Rivers Authority* (N.R.A.) - I.W. Sub District, based in Newport, manages water resources in the I.W. It measures river levels and flows using a series of recorders and monitors over fifty boreholes. It is constantly checking the quality of river water and (see under (v)) sampling tidal water quality on the bathing beaches for analysis to ensure compliance with EC standards.

The N.R.A. is also responsible for flood defences (both sea and river), river fisheries in the E.Yar and Medina although major environmental issues are controlled from Southern Regional H.Q. in Worthing.

(ii) *Supply* - The I.W. is well provided (no pun!) with underground water which, together with river abstraction, is supported by a back-up cross Solent service, laid between Fawley on the mainland and Gurnard, importing water from the R. Test as needed during the high season when the Island is full of visitors.

(iii) *Southern Water Services Ltd.* - This private Utility Company, serving the Isle of Wight supplies nearly 40 megalitres (9,000,000 gallons) of water, per day to meet the requirements of the Island. In this regard over 90% of I.W. properties are separately metered which has helped to reduce unnecessary wastage of water.

(iv) *The Mains Supply* - The network in the I.W. comes from the supply sources shown in Fig 88 which should be compared with the Geology map (Fig 2) and related to the porous chalk areas in the Island.

(v) *Tidal Water* - The protection of tidal water quality extends to a distance of three miles from the coast. In order to meet the requirements of the EC Bathing Water Directive, Southern Water will need to replace the shorter sea outfalls (see Fig 88); this is in hand.

(vi) *Waste* - Waste Water Treatment Works are being updated across the Island and earlier works are being abandoned as new construction projects replace the old. As an example of a small modern unit, the new system at St. Helens is capable of a treated waste water capacity of 1480m³/day.

UTILITIES

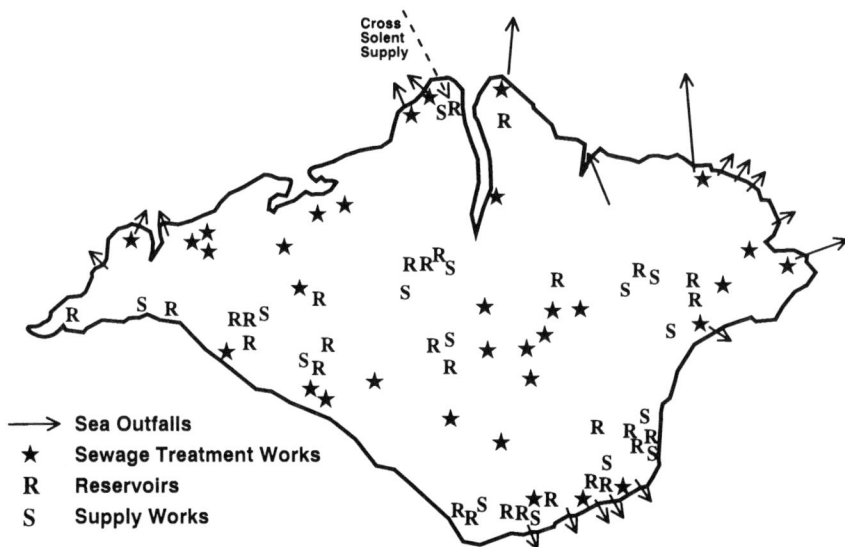

Sea Outfalls
★ **Sewage Treatment Works**
R **Reservoirs**
S **Supply Works**

Fig 88. I.W. - Water - Supply & Waste Systems

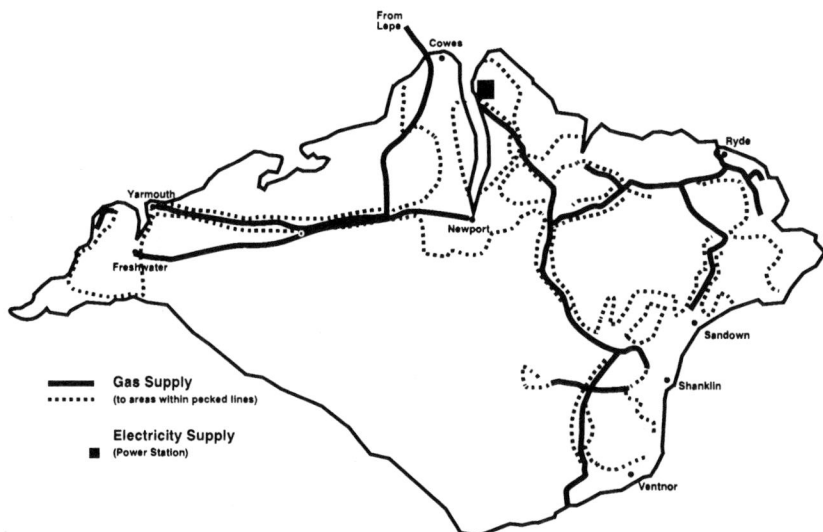

── **Gas Supply**
······ (to areas within pecked lines)

■ **Electricity Supply**
(Power Station)

Fig 89. I.W. - Energy - Gas & Electricity

In sequence, its processes cover the following operations, leaving pure, clear water at the end of the line:-

Inlet Works   -   mechanical screening

Primary settlement and Storm tanks

Filter Beds   -   Biological treatment

Humus tanks   -   solids drawn off

Sludge holding - tankered for treatment at Sandown

Note: The bulk of the 1626 tonnes (1600 tons) of sludge collected annually is used agriculturally; NO sludge from treatment works is dumped at sea.

(vii) At one time the control of water supply and waste was the responsibility of a variety of different authorities - notable among which was the Commissioner of Sewers in the 17th century. Thence, Local Authorities, Water Boards, River Boards etc. until, today, we have collective responsibility, properly monitored and all supervised from a control room in Newport, manned 24 hrs a day.

ENERGY
(b) *GAS*

(i) *Town Gas* was originally produced at the I.W. Gas Works central plant at Kingston, on the banks of the River Medina, at East Cowes. Although now closed as a gas works, it follows that the mains system as at first laid with its many interconnections is, nevertheless, still used for the piped gas supplies but - it must be noted - these supplies do NOT cover the whole Island. The variously sized mains carry gas at high, intermediate and medium pressure, including the use of one main laid under the R. Medina. There are two Gasometers (Holder Stations) in reserve at Kingston.

(ii) *Natural Gas* now comes to the Island from the mainland super-grid system, by pipeline from Lepe to Egypt Point, Cowes thence distributed by BRITISH GAS, TRANSCO, to the areas shown within the pecked lines in Fig 89.

(iii) *Bottled Gas* is used in the areas not supplied with natural gas and is conveyed by tanker for storage in private holding tanks.

(c) ELECTRICITY

(i) *Distribution in the I.W.* - Whereas the gas supply is only available in the more urban areas, electricity is readily available throughout the whole of the Island.

(ii) *Generation* - It is at present supplied by *National Power* from the *National Grid*, by cross-Solent undersea cables. It is augmented, locally, by power generated and derived from the I.W. Council Waste Plant, at Newport, from their non-fossil fuel pellets - through the supply network. This is a form of *Renewable Energy* - see sub para (vi) below. The Power Station at Kingston, East Cowes, is also kept available as a "top-up" supply facility but, more importantly, as an emergency source of energy supply in the event of isolation of power from the mainland.

(iii) *Transmission* - Is in the control of *Southern Electric*, Solent Division. Electricity is transmitted both by underground cable as well as overhead lines, as illustrated in Fig 89. Demand continues to rise rapidly each year - at a greater rate than the rise in population - thus reflecting the steadily increasing rate of individual consumption.

(d) RENEWABLE ENERGY SOURCES

It would be very satisfying to be able to record a variety of renewable energy sources at work in the I.W. Yet, close enquiry into the many alternatives does not promise great hope at the present time. Summarised, possibilities in the future are:-

(i) Hydro-Electric schemes - exploiting the Rivers Yar and Medina.

(ii) Geo-thermal energy - from deep below the ground.

(iii) Wave power - using energy from the sea around.

(iv) Solar power - harnessing and using the sun's heat (although, in this respect, the author is of the opinion that far more could be done in the Island on a smaller scale).

(v) Wind - use of the wind's generating potential is, perhaps, the most practicable measure - as an individual unit, in *clusters* or in a more commercial *wind farm;* the latter would however conflict with many I.W. *conservation* policies.

(vi) Lastly, mention has already been made of the existing non-fossil fuel energy source currently operating as in sub para c (ii) above.

45. ENVIRONMENT

(i) *"All this beauty is of God"* - Earlier in the book, mention was made of the "quality of life" in the I.W. Clearly, one of our most important assets which, daily, enhance that "quality" is - our *environment*. We live on a beautiful island amidst a rich tapestry of landscape. The map, (Fig 90 over), illustrates the large amount of conservation and coastal protection. These, together with its flora, fauna and archaeological interests, all combined with our sunny climate and social advantages (e.g. low crime rate, low pollution, peaceful neighbourhoods etc.) make for the enrichment of life. Early Geographers preached *"determinism"* in which it was said that "Man's actions were determined by his environment" - could that be true in the Island?

(ii) *The sketch map in Fig 90 shows* :-

Stretches of *Heritage Coast* extending for 45 kms (28 miles)
Areas of Outstanding Natural Beauty covering 50% of the Island
Forty *Sites of Special Scientific Interest*
Five local *Nature Reserves*

besides all the *Green Gaps* between different settlements and a note to see Fig 43, especially the forests and woodlands which cover another 9% of the Island, as well as many *National Trust* properties.

(iii) *Countryside* - Under EC reform the countryside is changing as an increasing amount of agricultural land is being set aside, sold or diversified in use. It is in the rural areas that population growth increases and more retired people are settling. Countryside stewardship is now helping to integrate protective measures for the landscape. Opportunities are greater for the increase of forestry, leisure and a multi-purpose countryside which is not entirely agricultural.

(iv) *Development* - All the foregoing change involves development and this must be coupled with the need for the Island's economic advance which can often lead to conflict with environmental programmes. Here in the I.W. we are fortunate to have a sound strategical Planning Structure and officers alive to the pressures involved.

Economic growth by itself is not enough since, by safeguarding the environment in the I.W., the source of much wealth is also being protected.

(v) *Recreational Horizons* - There is a link between sport and environmental planning and proposals such as coastal development of yachting, windsurfing, sea canoeing, water skiing and rowing added to the new framework "Strategy Plan" of inland physical activity, prepared by the I.W. Council, all help to provide a well structured environment.

(vi) *Archaeology* - The preservation of archaeological remains is a distinct element of the Island's environment, since they are both part of our cultural heritage and irreplaceable. Maritime sites also exist around our shores and a "Maritime Sites and Monuments Record" has been added to the remit of the County Archaeological Unit.

(vii) *Historic Parks* - English Heritage have compiled a register of gardens and parks of special historic interest which include, in the I.W.:-

Appuldurcombe, Norris Castle, Nunwell, Osborne, Swainston and Westover. The N.T. property, Mottistone Manor, which, as with a variety of other Manors, Nature Reserves, stone cottages, thatched dwellings etc. all help to enrich the environment.

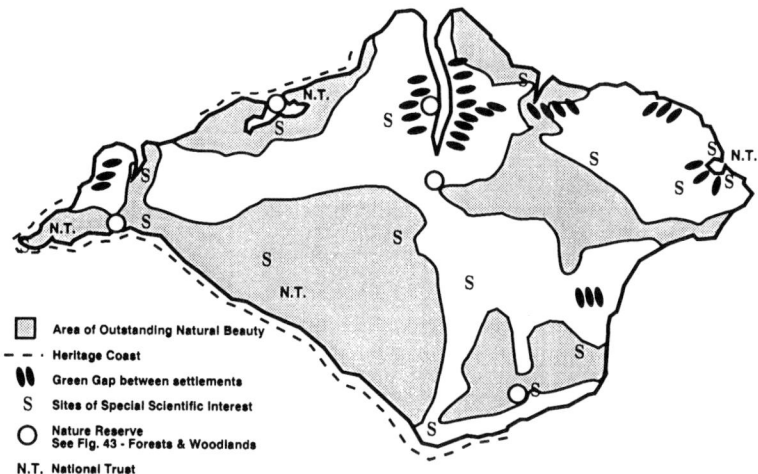

Area of Outstanding Natural Beauty
- - · Heritage Coast
Green Gap between settlements
S Sites of Special Scientific Interest
O Nature Reserve
See Fig. 43 - Forests & Woodlands
N.T. National Trust

Fig 90. I.W. Environment

46. ECONOMIC GEOGRAPHY

Economic Geography - a hybrid science, concerns the organisation of man and his wealth, commerce, transport and the whole system of exchanges and resources. Some would argue that **because it is an island** the I.W. does not receive its fair share of the Nation's resources.

Islands - compared with other islands, the I.W. is the exception in that:-

Isle of Man - is governed by the Tynwald, independent of much of Central Government, with its own revenues, including Customs and low rate of Income Tax.

Channel Isles - independently governed, as appointed by the various States with its own low rate of Income Tax

Scilly Isles - run by a Council, created by special Order of a Local Government Act and specially Grant Aided.

By contrast the I.W., in terms of population, is nearly twice as large as any of the above - with total expenditure and income probably greater despite the absence of any power to raise special revenues. In 1962 the then Ministry of Housing and Local Government issued a White Paper which, in the case of the ISLE OF WIGHT said -

"There is a prima facie case for weighting to take <u>full</u> account of the inevitably higher costs caused by severance from the mainland by sea"

NO real effect has been given to this conclusion!

The unique water barrier separating the I.W. from all other English counties has a significant effect on the economic profile of the Island. On the other hand, it is the very uniqueness of the Island that makes it the haven which separates it from many other problems experienced on the mainland. See also Appendix II for a sample Budget.

What are the I.W's current economic problems? Briefly they include:-

High unemployment - the Island's percentage rate is well ahead.

Imbalance in the population structure - increasing number of elderly.

Low employment growth - in spite of "Assisted Area" status.

Low economic activity - I.W. workers are some of the lowest paid.

Lack of investment - very little by way of large capital development.

Declining infrastructure - limited budgets increase neglect.

Where lies the remedy? - the politician's answer seems to lie somewhere between "We must have intervention/investment from the Government or European Community" and "Help!"

A Geographer's answer - look at the geographical and physical barriers, look at the low base from which the economy needs to develop, look at the present economic structure (primarily supported by the service sector - in which we do best, particularly tourism) with few secondary industries and fewer primary: then, look laterally and afresh at the direction in which we might travel that still preserves our chief resource - our environment.

Which way? - hopefully, the more discerning reader will have noted pointers en route leading to:-

Tourism - there is abundant scope for development in this area that recognises changing holiday habits and the huge potential in the Conference trade (see also Appendix IV, page 117).

Tax - if the Island cannot follow the other islands quoted above in raising revenue, surely so much could be done to benefit the whole Island by introducing a simple Landing Levy.

Tertiary industry - to avoid the costs of insularity can we not use the environmental bait, the postal service and Hi-Tec electronic communication to encourage the major national commercial company offices (insurance, pools etc.) which need people but little new development that might increase pollution? And - why not all out effort to obtain our own *"UNIVERSITY OF THE WIGHT"*?

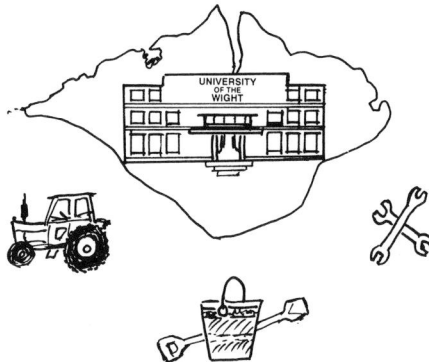

Fig 91. I.W. Economy

Apologia

In order, so far as possible, to maintain the format of matching the narrative with supporting visual data, this has often meant abrupt treatment of some of the more serious elements in this study. I am also aware that the level of content has oscillated in order to accommodate a number of important geographical ideas.

My apologies for this - as also to those of the fair sex for using "men" in the script which they will realise is no more than shorthand for "humankind".

So far as practicable the whole content has been written objectively although it spilled over into the subjective on page 94, in the final part of section 46 and, quite deliberately, in Appendix IV.

Summary

Except that it has no mountains, lakes, motorways or very large cities, the **ISLE OF WIGHT** is a microcosm of the U.K, albeit with a better climate.

It has much to offer in both the Physical and Human branches of Geography. This has been so evident in the teaching of young children, students and their teachers (of all ages and abilities - from primary to graduate levels) where example after example of geographical ideas to be learned or case studies to be quoted can be readily drawn from their knowledge and experiences in the I.W.

THE ISLAND is a beautiful place in which to live or visit on holiday and has woven a pattern and approach to life that is very much its own. I would hope that some of the writer's enthusiasm for "This Garden Isle" has rubbed off on to the reader. Particularly to those visitors who, I trust, have found that it's people's attitude to "overners" has been intelligent and always friendly.

I would hope, too, that this "Geographer's Look" has also helped to illuminate some of the many facets in this island jewel.

Glossary of Terms

For ease of reference, this glossary is arranged, alphabetically but in sequence - to follow the PAGE and SECTION numbers to which it refers: a word, once explained, is not repeated.

PAGE(S)   SECTION(S)
   16-18   **3**

Chalk - porous, sedimentary rock; mostly organic (shells etc.).
Clay - non porous sedimentary rock; a form of sticky mud.
Cretaceous - period in earth's history - see Table in Fig 3.
Drift - materials deposited on top of bedrock by wind or sea.
Folding - bending of the rock strata in the earth's crust.
Gravel - broken up small rock pebbles.
Lignite - compacted vegetable matter, between peat and coal
Marine - to do with the sea
Outcrop - bedrock that is visible on the surface of the earth
Palaeogene } see Table in Fig 3 - more recent
Pleistocene } periods in the earth's history
Raised beach - ancient beach lifted up by earth movements, above sea level
Relief - shape of the earth's surface
Rocks - material forming the hard crust of the earth
  Strata - layer (N.B. - the lowest being the oldest rock)
Sand - fine, gritty particles of broken rock
Sedimentary - rocks deposited in layers by wind, ice or water
Wealden - very early period in earth's history; see Fig 3
   19-20   **4 -5**
Angle of Dip - vertical angle of rock stratum
Anticline - arch-like fold of earth's crust
Erosion - wearing away of the land surface by wind, ice & water
Geology - science dealing with history of the earth's crust
  Structure - the way in which the rocks are arranged
Horizontal - parallel with the horizon
  Bedded - rock strata laid down in separate planes
  Bedrock - the solid rock lying under the topsoil or subsoil
Syncline - the trough of a fold in the earth's crust
Vale - valley between hills or cuestas
   21-23   **6-7**
Altitude - height above mean sea level
Bay - wide curved inlet of the sea or a lake
Cliff - high, steep precipice along a coast, river or lake

21-23	**6-7** (cont.)
Dissected	- erosion of land surface by rivers
Dry Valley	- a valley no longer containing permanent water
Headland	- a cape ending in a steep cliff
Impermeable -	will not allow water to pass through (non porous)
Landslip	- mass downward movement of earth material by gravity
Pervious	- will permit water to pass through (porous)
River Gap	- a break in a ridge cut by a river stream
Scarp (or Escarpment) - steep front slope of a cuesta
Terraces	- pairs or a series of steps in a high, steep slope
Topography -	detailed description of a locality and its features
Water Table -	upper level of water saturation (usually underground)
Weathering -	processes by which rocks are disintegrated

25-26   8

Rivers
- are said to "rise" at their "source" (start) and flow down towards their "mouth", where tides come in and out. "Estuaries" are created by a rise in sea level and are shaped like a funnel.
- are fed by "tributaries" from within their "catchment area" which is bounded by its "watershed".
- in "Trellis" drainage , tributaries of the main river extend their valleys by "headward" erosion into the vales. Thus, the principal river flowing down the slope (Consequent) is fed by streams called Subsequent rivers.
- sometimes the upper waters are diverted to another river stream with more powerful erosion - this is called "River Capture"
- "Run-off" is the total discharge of all water i.e. the rate it flows out from a drainage area.
- "Tidal sluices" are a type of gate that controls the flow of water out at the point where it meets the sea
- the area next to a river which overflows its banks and on which alluvium is deposited is called the "flood plain".

Chine   - a cleft or small canyon, found in the I.W.

28   10

Knick Point	- a break in the long profile of a stream
Meander	- a curve of a an old, mature river
Rejuvenated -	made young again
Truncated	- cut off

30   13

Backwash	- undertow of a receding wave
Deposition	- laying down of material particles, carried along
Groynes	- a wall of wood, concrete etc. to trap longshore drift
Load	- material carried by wind, waves, ice or rivers

Longshore Drift - movement of material along the shore, by waves
Swash   -   rush of water up a beach after a wave has broken
                   14
Graded   -   sorted out into different sizes
High Water   -   the time when the tide is at its full
Low Water   -   when the tide is furthest from the coastline
Storm beach   -   a beach covered with material from storm waves
                   15
Arches   -   openings through a mass of rock
Caves   -   hollows in the cliffs or underground
Stacks   -   steep, bare pillars of rock on a sea coast
Wave-cut   -   Platform - a shelf formed along a coast by wave erosion
                       Notch - narrow cut at base of a sea cliff, by waves
     31   **17**
Isthmus   -   narrow stretch of land joining larger areas
Peninsula   -   long, narrow stretch of land projecting out into sea
     33   **17**
Scouring   -   powerful erosive action of a current or flow of water
Silting   -   settling of sedimentary materials
Stranded   -   left isolated
                   18
Ebb   -   outgoing tidal stream or falling tide
Fathom   -   a unit of six feet, used by sailors in soundings
Soundings   -   recorded depth of water below chart datum
     35   **19**
G.M.T.   -   the local time at Greenwich, used for U.K. standard time
Tides   -   Low (Lowest is "Neap") when least high
                       High (Highest is "Spring") when at greatest height
Range   -   the difference in levels between High and Low tides
     36   **20**
Weather   -   daily conditions of wind, sun, rain, temperature etc.
Weather Statistics - collected numerical facts, arranged tidily
                   21
Climate   -   summary average of all weather measurements over time
Iso   -   a prefix used to denote lines of equal value; examples:-
  Isobars   -   equal atmospheric pressure
  Isohel   -   equal sunshine
  Isoneph   -   equal cloudiness
  Isotherm   -   equal temperature
  Isohyets   -   equal rainfall

	38	22
Alluvium	-	fertile deposits (sand, silt etc.) by a river
Soil types	-	Brown earth; good agricultural loam with humus
		Black earth (Chernozem) fertile with humus & lime
		Loess - yellowish soil particles, blown by the wind
		Loam - mixture of clay, sand and vegetable matter
		Peat - decomposed vegetable matter
		Podsol- greyish white soil, acidic; cool countries
Soil Profile	-	succession of soil layers (or Horizons) "A", "B" & "C"

Temperate Zone - lying between Tropic of Cancer and Arctic Circle

	38	23
Urban	-	relating to a town or city
Rural	-	relating to the countryside
	40	24
Coniferous	-	evergreen trees, produce "softwood"
Deciduous	-	trees that lose their leaves in Winter
		25
Cycles	-	systematic succession of changes
Ecosystem	-	unit of animals, plants & the environment
Fauna	-	animal life
Flora	-	plant life

Flows (as in script) - direction of movement in a line

Network	pattern of lines (links) for analysis
Systems	- structured, related set of objects

	41	27
Arable	-	cultivation of crops (not pasture or woodland)

Contour Ploughing - level rather than up and down the slope

Dairy	-	keeping cattle for milk
Horticulture	-	growing flowers, fruit and vegetables
Mixed	-	rearing animals and growing crops on the same farm
Poultry	-	raising domestic fowls
Viticulture	-	cultivation of vines (growing grapes for wine)

	43-45	29

Cottage Industry - items made in the homes of people
Craft Industries - artistic articles made by experts
Estates (Industrial) - places where smaller firms operate together
Light Industry - making smaller items with little raw materials
Heavy Industry - making big bulk items, using many raw materials
Manufacturing - processing raw materials, with machines

	47	31a
Factors	-	all the separate and important items, completing a result

Secondary Source Material - information obtained from another place

49   31b
Trails   - organised walks along particular routes
49   31c
County Town- the chief town (Capital) of the County
Ferry Port   - place where ferry vessels can berth, load and unload
Holiday Town   - a town organised to attract holidaymakers
Spa Town   - a health resort, developed from medicinal springs
50   31d
Behavioural Geography - a branch of Human geographical studies
Conference   - a large group of people meeting for discussion
Model   - theoretical example, designed for analysis and synthesis
Socio-economic - division of people according to a formulae (Appendix II)
51   31d
Construction Industry - building in general
Employment - direct; work immediately concerned on the spot
                   indirect; work associated with other work
Invisible Export (in tourism) - money which foreigners spend in U.K.
Multiplier Effect - where one item leads to another
Package Holidays - where all travel, accommodation etc. is unified
52   31e
Economic Geography - section dealing with economic/place factors
53   32b
Nationalised - taken over by the Government; public ownership
Transport   - L.R.T. System; modern travel on rails (double or single); or
                    overhead power lines
55   32c
Turnpikes   - earlier form of toll or payment to use road
32d
Floating Bridge - flat vessel that hauls across river on chains
32e
Bridleways   - tracks used by horse-riders
58   33
Anthropology - study of the peoples of the world and their habits
Ethnology   - scientific study of the races and their distribution
Population Density - the total number of people living in an area
Social Science - part of Human Geography studying whole of society
Statistician - one who records and analyses numerical facts
61   33d
Birth Rate   - the number of live births for every 1,000 persons
Death Rate   - the number of deaths for every 1,000 persons
Natural Increase/Decrease - differences between Birth/Death rates

61   33f

Emigration - movement of people out, to settle in another country

Immigration - movement of people into a country, to settle down

Migration - movement of people from one place to another

62   34

Housing - detached; separate, in its own grounds
flats; set of rooms in a building, usually on one floor

Household - collective total of all persons in the house

Second Home- place kept for holiday use beside the usual home

Urban Geography - study of towns, cities and their many functions

64   35d

Industry - work organised as a profit making activity

Trade - commercial buying and selling

65   37a/d

Relationships - how one thing connects with another

Settlements, in order of size-

  Homestead - a single dwelling

  Hamlet - a cluster of houses in the countryside

  Village - a small, rural settlement, small population

  Town - a compact urban settlement, larger population

Settlements - functions (or the part they play)

  Administrative - place of all the management activities

  Capital - chief centre, usually with County/Town Hall

  Commerce/Shopping - business of buying and selling

  Services - providing for the community

Subsistence - growing crops for own use but not enough to sell

70   37g

Central Business District - term used to describe the city centre

Decaying - breaking up, falling into disuse

Rejuvenated - brought to life again, modernised

Urban Structure - the manner in which the township is arranged

Borough - a form of local government, between County and Parish

72   37i

Sea-mark - a recognisable point of reference, viewed from the sea

73

Biogeography - study of plants and animals and their distribution

Markets - the place where goods are sold from stalls

75   38

Mail order - the purchase of goods by post

76   39

Local authorities - the local government, as in section 39b

Charter - Royal document granting various rights and privileges

76   39 (cont.)

Coat of Arms - an heraldic badge
80   40

Central Government - legislature of the U.K., "Parliament"
Electoral Ward - the area which elects one representative Councillor
I.W. Council - the governing body for the whole of the I.W.
Parish/Town Council - the elected body for a small local area
Unitary Authority - the 48 seat assembly that replaces previous Local Authorities
84   42a

"Neighbourhood Watch" - Households "self-help" Community Scheme
90   44c

Renewable resource - which can be replaced (e.g. trees) by planting
Renewable energy - power from sun, water, wind etc.
44d

Conservation - protection of the natural environment for the future
Wind   - clusters; small groups of wind turbines
                  - farm; a battery of wind turbines
91   45

Environment - all surrounding natural phenomena, untouched by man
  Green Gaps - land free of building, between settlements
  Heritage Coast - area of nationally important undeveloped coastline
National Trust - owns and controls land and properties in the U.K.
  In the I.W. these include :-
  West Wight -   Afton, Brook, Compton & Tennyson Downs, Brook, Compton
                 & Shippards Chines
  Bembridge - 18th century windmill
  Borthwood - woodland area
  St. Helens - The Duver and former Royal I.W. Golf Links
  Ventnor   - Bonchurch & St. Boniface Downs
                 and numerous properties (e.g. Mottistone Manor, Newtown old
                 Town Hall)
AONB   - nationally important landscape areas
SSSI   - important nature reserves; areas for flora and fauna
Monuments - ancient archaeological sites e.g. Longstone, Pepper Pot etc.

Appendix I

A. BIBLIOGRAPHY

Much of the content of this book has been drawn from the author's Teaching Notes acquired over the years, as well as from the Census Atlas, 1991.

Although little, true, geographical reading is available, there is a great deal of interesting I.W. material obtainable from the County Libraries in addition to the book-shops.

Some use has also been made of the following:-

E. DU BOULAY	Bembridge Past and Present 1911 - *B.S.C.*
B. DICKS	The Isle of Wight 1979 - *David & Charles*
D.E.S.	Geography in the National Curriculum 1994 - *H.M.S.O.* Geologist Association Guide No.25 1966 - *Benham & Co. Ltd.*
R. HOLLIS	Brading Haven - a Geographical study 1963 - *(Unpublished)*
ISLAND PLANNING UNIT	Census Atlas 1991 I.W. Structure Plan - Draft 1994 Island 2000 - Background Papers 1994
I.G.S.	Short Account of the Geology of the I.W. 1968 - *H.M.S.O.*
J. LOVELOCK	GAIA Practical Science of Planetary Medicine - *GAIA Books Ltd.*
C. ASPINALL - OGLANDER	Nunwell Symphony 1945 - *Hogarth Press*
L. WILSON	Portrait of the I.W. 1965 - *Robert Hale*

USEFUL ADDRESSES
I.W. Associations, 1995, (N.B. prefix "I.W." not shown)

Botanical Gardens	M. Crump	36 St. John's Road Newport	527606
Citizens Advice Bureau		17 Quay Street Newport	522611
C.P.R.E.	Mrs E. Whitehead	Wootton Bridge	882165
Country Landowners	Col. K. Shapland	Grove House Yarmouth	760729
Countryside Mgt.	I. Rowat	41 Sea Street Newport	822119
County Press (Island Index)		123 Pyle Street Newport	825333
Cultural Services & Library H.Q.		Parkhurst Newport	823822
Development Board		117 High Street Newport	826222
Enterprise Agency		6 Town Lane Newport	529120
Geological Museum	Curator	High Street Sandown	404344
Historical Assocn.	Mrs M. Pewsey	56 New Road Brading	407300
Horticultural Assocn	Miss M. Walden	Oak Cottage Shorwell	740207
National Farmers Union		8 Gunville Rd. Newport	522996
National Trust		35a St James's St. Newport	526445
Natural History & Archy.		Rylstone Gdns Shanklin	740289
Places of Interest	R. Young	Haseley Manor Arreton	865420
Ramblers Assocn.	Ms. G. Wardle	Ryde	566726
Society	J. Barnes	51 Cambridge Rd E. Cowes	293010
Sports & Recreation	G. Moglione	Stables Church Rd Cowes	292545
Steam Railway		Havenstreet Ryde	882204
Tourism		Quay Side Newport	524343
Tourist Industry Assocn.	D. Wood		563168
Trails (Brochure from Tourist Info)		Parkhurst Forest	522583

TRAVEL

Hovertravel		Ryde	811000
Red Funnel		Cowes	292101
Southern Vectis		Newport	826826
Wightlink		Portsmouth	(01705) 827744
Weather Data	Met. Office	160 High St. Southampton	
			(01703) 228844
Wildlife Trust	Dr. Pope	Forest Rd Newport	522949

NOTE - The Customer Service Centre, I.W. Council (A-Z facilities)   823200

Appendix II

STATISTICAL DATA

In large part the material following has been obtained from the **CENSUS 1991** and with the help of the Island Planning Unit. As with the Glossary, for ease of reference this information is listed under the Page and Section numbers to which it refers.

Page 38 - Section 23

LAND USE

Area	38.014 ha	146.8 sq.mls.
Forest	3,240 ha	12.5 sq.mls.
Farmed	25,809 ha	99.6 sq.mls.
Roads	787 kms.	489.0 mls.
F/pths	830 kms.	515.8 mls.
Rivers	20 kms.	12.5 mls.
Developed	5,180 ha	20.0 sq.mls.

PROTECTED AREAS

AONB	19,038 ha	73.3 sq.mls.
SSSI	3,072 ha	11.9 sq.mls.
Heritage Coast	45 kms.	28 mls.

Page 41 - Section 27

FARMING

USE - hectares	**1981**	**1991**	
Grassland	13,417	12,274	
Grazing	1,923	1,516	
Woodland	774	1,085	
Crops	10,046	10,175	
Set aside	503	759	
TOTAL	**26,664**	**25,809**	
FARM TYPES - Nos.			
Dairy	120	83	
Livestock	40	45	(cattle - sheep +)
Pigs/Poultry	9	2	
Crops	26	40	
Vegetables	5	3	
Fruit	4	9	
Horticulture	40	32	
Mixed	6	6	
Part-time	227	294	

CROP TYPES - areas in hectares

Wheat	3,807	5,035
Barley	4,382	1,521
Oats	401	175
Other cereals	3	134
Beans & Peas	95	617
Rape (Oilseed)	89	1,133
Potatoes	274	207
Other crops	405	857

FARM SIZES - Nos.

0 - 10 hectares	145	194
10 - 50 hectares	201	183
50 -200 hectares	109	115
Over 200 hectares	22	22
TOTAL	**477**	**514**

Page 43 - Section 29

I.W. INDUSTRIAL ESTATES Company Types (examples) & Nos.

Utilities	-	Service companies	5
Garages	-	Car sales and repairs	20
Storage		(Warehousing) & Distribution (Tpt.)	48
General	-	Manufacturing & Prodn.	44
Light Industry	-	Electl,Fabricn,Food etc.	45
Retail/Wholesale	-	Building,Catering,Electl,Farmg,Caravans etc.	52

Latest information indicates that there is currently 85 hectares (210 acres) of undeveloped landallocated/available for industry.

Page 51 - Section 31d

TOURISM

TIME OF HOLIDAY (%s)	ALL	STAYING	DAY TRIPPERS
Early (pre June)	14	18	8
Peak (July/August)	69	63	77
Late (post Sept)	17	19	15
Previous Visits - YES	62	54	68
NO	32	40	28

LENGTH OF STAY	NIGHTS	WEEKS
	1-2 (16%)	ONE 49%
	3-4 (11%)	TWO 18%
	5-6 (6%)	

HOLIDAYMAKERS - characteristics

Single	9%	Couples	35%
Groups (5+)	18%	Parents with Children	38%

ACCOMMODATION - types used
Hotels,Guest Houses etc   34%
Self Catering (inc Campg.) 35%
Holiday Camps   8%
Relatives & Friends   13%
Other   10%
Currently estimated - 2,000 tourist establishments available with accommodation for over 62,000 persons

Page 55 - Section 32c
COMMUNICATIONS

ROADS	Kms	Miles	REGISTERED
"A"	122.3	76.0	VEHICLES (Estd)
Others	664.7	413.0	Cars & Vans 50,000
			H.G.V.s 3,000
TOTALS	**787**	**489**	**Others 10,000**

Page 56 - Section 36g
SEA
Trans-Solent Services, from:-

Port	Service	No.	Capacity (Persons)	(Cars)
RYDE	Hovercraft	2	96	
	Catamaran	2	450	
FISHBOURNE	RoRo	4	1000	142
E.COWES	RoRo	3	850	85
W.COWES	Hydrofoil	4	67	
	Catamaran	2	120	
YARMOUTH	RoRo	3	756	58

CROSSINGS - ALL routes (Annual total 1991)

Passengers	7,375,238
Cars	1,084,200
Coaches	17,088
Commercial	183,280

Page 58 - Section 33a
POPULATION GROWTH
Actual & Forecast

1801	22,000
1821	31,500
1841	42,500
1861	55,000
1881	73,500
1901	82,500
1921	85,000
1931	88,500
1951	95,500
1971	107,000
1981	122,000
1991	126,300
1994	124,700

Forecast - adjusted

1996	126,600
2006	129,700
2011	130,100

Page 62 - Section 34
HOUSEHOLDS

Composition	I.W.	G.B.
Living alone	28.1	10.6
Married	33.4	23.6
(& children)	17.6	40.8
Lone (& child)	3.5	6.5
Others	17.4	18.4

DWELLINGS

Detached	37.1	20.2
Semi-det.	27.6	29.2
Terraced	16.5	29.3
Flat	18.7	21.2
Bed-sit	0.2	0.1

Page 58 - Section 33a
CHANGES - Forecast
Ages   All (0-85+)

Dates	1991	1996	2001	2011
Nos (000s)	125	127	129	130

OVER THE LAST TEN YEARS -
Comparison

85+	+ 65%
75-84	+ 24
65-74	- 4
55-64	- 4
45-54	+ 20
20-44	+ 12
16-19	- 9
0-15	- 5
All	+ 6

Page 61 - Section 33e
ETHNIC GROUPS in I.W. - Nos.

African, Caribbean	278
Indian	117
Pakistan	18
Bangladeshi	37
Chinese	103
Asian	110
Eirean	1,131
Others	247
White	123,667

TENURE	I.W.	G.B.
Owner occupied	79.8%	66.3%
Rented - private	8.7	7.1
Rented Local Authy	12.4	26.5

Page 62 - Section 35a

EMPLOYMENT - Comparative 10% sample of I.W./G.B.Occupations

TYPE	I.W. Nos.	I.W. %	G.B. %
Professional/Local Govt.	190	4.0	6.6
Educn, Health, Welfare	482	10.2	9.3
Literary, Art & Sports	48	1.0	1.3
Science, Engineering, Techy.	221	4.7	4.8
Managerial	667	14.1	12.1
Clerical & related	621	13.1	16.6
Selling	327	6.9	6.2
Security & protection	138	2.9	2.1
Catering & personal services	708	15.0	11.0
Farming, Fishing etc.	95	2.0	1.3
Materials processing	242	5.1	6.0
Electl, & Metal	405	8.6	8.8
Decorating, Assembling etc.	120	2.5	3.2
Construction, Mining etc.	216	4.6	3.2
Transport, Storage etc.	155	3.3	5.5
Miscellaneous	88	1.9	2.0
TOTAL - ALL OCCUPATIONS (10%)	4,723	100.0	100.0

Page 81 - Section 41a

SOCIAL GEOGRAPHY

EDUCATION   SCHOOLS

Ages	5-9	9-13	13-18	Private	Special
Number	46	16	5	4	2
Pupils	6,867	5,320	4,874	1,239	-
Teachers	362	296	348	-	-

F.E.- I.W. College of Arts & Technology (600 staff, 200 courses)

SCHOOL POPULATION - Forecast Nos.

Type	1995	2000	
Primary	7,250	8,400	falling
Middle	5,800	6,300	static
High	5,300	5,900	static

Page 83 - Section 41b

HEALTH - facilities include the services of:-

General Practitioners	70	Homes for the Elderly
Dental Practitioners	47	Bedspaces 2,000
Opticians	22	

Page 93 - Section 46
ECONOMIC - The I.W.Council's Budget Estimate 1995-96
A.Where does the money come from?

Grant from Central Govt.	£40,369,000	(£323.54 per head)
Non-Domestic Rates	£26,855,000	(£215.23 per head)
Council Tax (see *)	£25,733,000	(£206.24 per head)
TOTAL	**£92,957,000**	**(£745.01 per head)**

B.Where does it go?

Service	Net Expenditure
Education	£48,061,000
Social Services	£14,535,000
Housing	£577,000
Highways	£5,708,000
Fire	£3,945,000
Refuse	£3,044,000
Environment	£730,000
Recreation/Tourism	£3,683,000
Planning/Develpt.	£1,584,000
Other services	£11,090,000
TOTAL	**£92,957,000**

C.What besides?
To the above must be added/included
Local PARISH/TOWN COUNCIL levy) both of which vary*
Separate POLICE AUTHORITY levy)
D.Why the variation*?
The independent valuation on each PROPERTY determines the BAND of Council
Tax payable, where
Band A (property value 1991, up to £40,000) rises to
Band H property value over £320,000, with
Band D - the average, paying :-

	I.W.Council	£537.50
	Police	45.00
plus, say,	Parish (Chale)	7.40
	TOTAL	**£589.90**

E. So,I still don't understand!
Or, I think I'm able to obtain BENEFIT ? Then, refer back to page 81, section
40b(ii).

Appendix III

NOTES ON FIELDWORK

A valuable and interesting part of Geography is to study the local landscape within a small area - be it the coast, a farmstead, a cuesta or some aspect of urban geography, such as a village or town or whatever?

Whether you are a holidaymaker or student make it FUN but heed these few basic ideas :-

1. ALWAYS carry a MAP (if you are keen, a geology map as well) so that you can note, accurately, each Grid Reference point.

2. AS A HOLIDAYMAKER a simple NOTEBOOK will do but, for the student, you should have:-

> A base board and clip, with card or transparent cover
> Pencils (rather than pens), sharpener and a soft rubber
> Large plastic cover or clear bag - to keep rain off work
> Another bag to collect any specimens e.g. rock samples
> *Optional* - A camera - which saves time and gives accuracy
> A pair of field glasses if available.

3. DO NOT RELY ON YOUR MEMORY - write it down. When read again does it satisfy the 3Cs? Is it Clear, is it Concise, is it Complete? There is no, need to write sentences - simple notes, facts or headings will do.

4. KNOW WHERE IT IS? Whatever you draw - it must have a name or title, a compass direction, scale and be well annotated (labelled) so that, at some future date it can be instantly remembered.

5. FORGET SOPHISTICATION - you are more likely to finish up with a good field sketch if you can imagine looking out of a window and drawing exactly what a child sees.

6. DON'T BE afraid to change your vantage point; orientate your map and relate to the specific as well as the general. Share out the work and keep to a programme.

7. Block diagrams and Cross Sections can help to explain some points of detail. A Transect is another useful method.

8. Finally, remember you are acting as a GEOGRAPHER not as an artist and, thus, your objectives should lead to a better understanding of Geographical modes of enquiry , i.e.:-

> To observe, to think and to acquire knowledge
> To understand relationships between physical features and human activities
> To associate all the different phenomena comprising the whole geography of the area under scrutiny and an awareness of the problems raised.

9. Since most Field Work is part of an on-going Topic Study it is often helpful to evaluate in advance the skills and techniques to be used, the type of information data to be collected and the organisation necessary to complete your goal within a set time limit: this simple preparatory measure saves procrastination, indecision and "waffle"!

10. SOME convenient categories in Field Work include the following and, to be of real Geographical value, should be in the form of an enquiry that can subsequently be analysed, as a result of basic study <u>on the spot and in the field</u>:-

Architecture and Buildings	Industry & Commerce
Beaches and Coasts	Land Use - Agriculture/Farming
Climate and Meteorology	- Industrial
Conservation and Environment	Natural Vegetation
Communications	Physical features
Drainage (and Rivers)	Recreation
Flora and Fauna	Rural Studies
Geology	Settlement patterns
Geomorphology	Soils and Erosion
Harbours & Creeks	Urban studies

There are many others - the Author's Field Notebooks are full!

Appendix IV

POSTSCRIPT - The Future ISLE OF WIGHT - What?

All the foregoing summary of some of the many geographical horizons which comprise the Isle of Wight largely reflect the author's look out into physical **space** and the human activities of **place** <u>as at today</u> - scientific facts measured and described.

Now, as a final postscript, he has been advised to abstract the reader from all the previous objective and systematic study and, in the tiniest glimpse, look subjectively ahead into **time**! Except that the Geographer ordinarily deals with the past, leading up to the "here and now", it is a challenge for his enquiring mind to look into the future. The vision of what may lie ahead should help to perceive the chain of connection as it unrolls tomorrow.

So, let us examine this exploratory expedition into the uncharted waters of prophecy. Can we, for example, look back to the I.W. of a century ago in both the Physical and Human areas - follow its measured passage through until now and, thence, on into the 21st century?

However precisely recorded, can we project the empirical factual data of the past and interpolate its pointers with enough disciplined focus forward with any hint of accuracy? Can we identify potential change and, more particularly, the rate of that change? Could we say, for example (see Fig 56) that, because the population in 1801 was 20,000, in 1901 it was 80,000 and in 2001 is expected to be around 130,000 therefore, *per se*, in the year 2100 it will be of the order of 170,000? Clearly not! Navigation into the geographical future of the I.W. is not an exact science. Thus, treading into the unknown and always recognising the dynamics of modern geography - as compared with the static Victorian approach - what do we see changing in the years ahead?

PHYSICAL GEOGRAPHY

Let us first look again at the PHYSICAL GEOGRAPHY of this isle, starting with the key sections - EROSION (page 23), LANDSLIPS and SLIDES (page 28) and the COASTLINE (page 30) all part of the continuing process of destruction, modifying the shape of the Island, called DENUDATION.

Hopefully, most of the stacks forming the "Needles" should still be in place in a hundred years time although if the sea level rose they could, like much of the whole I.W. coastline, alter in shape. An estimate of the likely amount of change can be worked out from the figures given earlier in the book, <u>so long as similar climatic conditions , as now, prevail</u> (but - note under "Changes Ahead", over).

Here, though, we come upon the most unpredictable element in our look into the crystal ball - the pattern of WEATHER and CLIMATE to come? We have already seen (Section 17, sub para 2) how one dramatic storm completely changed the harbour entrance shape of Brading Haven virtually overnight.

GLOBAL WARMING

The creative scientist James Lovelock's GAIA hypothesis led to the discovery of the global build-up of fluorocarbons - critical to both the Greenhouse Effect and the much publicised Ozone Layer - in which "enlarged holes" are still currently occupying scientific attention. Lovelock suggests either a jump to a tropical ice-free earth or, to another Ice Age; on balance, by juggling his CO_2 figures, he postulates a rise in the mean temperature of 2.5°C within the next decade! Whilst the author does not personally agree with this figure, if we are to accept the ideas behind Lovelock's interpretation of GLOBAL WARMING - and we certainly should do so as the greenhouse gases are continuosly increasing, it then becomes a matter of judgment on what the consequences might be in the I. W. in the future.

On present knowledge we could speculate considerable rises in, both, the MEAN TEMPERATURE and the MEAN SEA LEVEL in the next few hundred years. But, having stated that, we cannot be sure that such rises will in fact occur - other than in theory - since there is little real evidence to show that the increased amount of carbon dioxide, nitrous oxide, methane and CFCs over the last century have materially changed our lives very much so far. Is "GAIA's" negative feedback at work? Yet, new sources of warmth have already opened ice barriers, for example between Spitzbergen and Greenland, and melted polar ice etc. which it would be churlish to ignore. Such rises in temperature must therefore imply rises in sea level. We would also do well to remember that we are currently in an "inter-glacial" period, that it was the "warming effect" that brought about the very existence of the I.W. in the first place (see page 25) and at present we are also in a warming cycle of the Sun's activity.

Although the precise effects of GLOBAL and increasing SOLAR WARMING on the I. W. are far from clear, the easy way to predict change would be to produce the "at best" and "at worst" scenarios and then leave the reader to decide! Would he agree with the author's conjecture, as under?

CHANGES AHEAD

Temperature - Whilst no dramatic change is likely in the next fifty years, steady and gradual moderation of the **CLIMATE** can be anticipated leading towards an eventual **Mediterranean** type of weather pattern before the end of the next millennium, with a <u>mean rise between</u> 1.5°C to 2°C by the end of the next century.

Sea Level - Our calculations on the potential rise in sea level suggest <u>no more than 2.5 - 5.0 cms (1-2 ins)</u> in the next100 years but, thereafter, an increasing rate eventually leading to the position postulated in the year 3,000 A.D. (see Fig 13 on page 22) which suggests a rise of up to 3 metres (10 feet).

Effects - the forecast changes in the I.W. could well be:-

CLIMATE - A gradual move towards hotter summers with less overall rainfall and warmer winters.

SEA LEVEL

Deposition - NO effect on the continuing build up of Ryde sandbanks, Bembridge spit etc.

Degradation - Will continue, as already forecast (Page 30) and, particularly, on the Chine coast between Blackgang and the Needles.

Drowning & Flooding - Will produce ever increasing problems in the three river valleys, the creeks at Newtown and Wootton also in the known low lying areas at Cowes, Freshwater, Ryde and Seaview.

A much closer watch will need to be kept on COASTAL PROTECTION and, it follows, further development in low lying areas may well have to be curtailed; dykes could become common place around waterfront buildings as, although uncertain exactly when, **RISING SEA LEVEL IS TO BE EXPECTED** as a problem of some magnitude in the centuries that lie ahead.

HUMAN GEOGRAPHY

"There's n'owt so queer as folk" is a truism indeed that must be recognised when attempting to estimate their passage through and on into the next century. However, since people and their activities are the very bread and butter basis of HUMAN GEOGRAPHY, what are the likely parameters in the I.W.? Here, the author concentrates on those areas of change which he believes are probable - as distinct from those which are desirable; these two factors are not necessarily complementary.

Instead of philosophising on health, wealth and happiness etc. be mindful that this is a "Geographer's Look" and thus we quickly return to a geographical nomenclature that follows the order established in the previous Part Four - but, with comment only where change of any significance is forecast in the next century.

INDUSTRY

General - Real growth can be expected in the TERTIARY sector, more limited and even reducing SECONDARY activities seem likely whereas progress in some areas of the PRIMARY sector seem ripe for change.

PRIMARY SECTOR

Agriculture and Farming - already, on page 41, we have noted the remarkable development in the Island. In the future we can expect further change as a result of simple economics and the increasing environmentally and health conscious age that is around the next corner.

Economically, the departure is foreseen of most if not all of the remaining small farms in favour of much larger co-operatives concentrating on high value crops: such bodies operating in groups, each farming in excess of 1,620 ha (4,000 acres).

With the desire for "healthier living" and the growth of vegetarianism, there will be a move away from cattle. Although present organic produce will remain a niche market, high value grain, potato and vegetable crops will support rape and linseed. Lupin and sunflower seed crops will be shortly added as soon as temperatures rise later on. The present lucrative subsidies and set aside payments which do not encourage maximum yields from the land may well lead to farmers diversifying into variations of the Tourist industry. Under the new Integrated Crop Management technique farmers will rely increasingly on their computers, fed by satellite, to run their old style crop - rotation, using less chemicals - much to the delight of both the "green" pressure groups and the R.S.P.B.

Quarrying - the land-won minerals available are adequate to meet market needs for some years to come but, as with marine dredging, their extraction is likely to be over-ruled by the environmentalists, thus requiring use of substitute aggregate or imported materials. Building and Road Engineering costs will therefore probably increase.

Exploration - it is highly possible that within the next century Oil and Gas supplies will be located close offshore. Such development would eventually bring an economic harvest to the I.W. as well as much political quarrelling.

Theoretically, regard would be given to A.O.N.B, S.S.I. and the Heritage Coast - it remains to be seen! Should such an off-shore field in the area lead to the extraction of methane gas in any quantity this could well cause sea bed subsidence. In turn, this could add to the problems of coastal protection, referred earlier.

SECONDARY SECTOR

The only way that the I.W. is likely to attract further manufacturing industry is to encourage "small bulk, high value" production that, because of the 'severance by sea' factor, limits high transport costs. In effect this probably requires travel along the information highway and the world of the micro-chip and its derivatives. A link bridge would be advantageous to industry.

Unless would-be entrepreneurs can be bribed or persuaded by the merits of operating in the Island's wholesome environment, there seem few growth prospects in the secondary sector other than in support of the Island's very own specialities (e.g. windsurfing, hang gliders, etc). and the equipment and clothing for each.

Except as above or in connection with any future bumper E.C. help or Oil/Gas developments, little change is forecast apart from the successful small-scale light industrial ventures still growing on the various Trading Estates and the continuance of the boat-building and associated yacht trade in all its many forms.

TERTIARY SECTOR
Commerce

Sadly, "Superstore Culture" has brought about the demise of too many High Street businesses and all the spin-off problems; the situation seems unlikely to improve very much in the coming decades. In this, Newport gains over Ryde.

Tourism

In the author's opinion, this is undoubtedly the area of economic activity that could show the greatest material change in the years ahead. The nature of the change(s) will depend on:-

(a) The industry, itself and collectively, under the aegis of a joint I.W. Council and, paramount, an <u>Island based</u> Tourist Board, working to a long term Development Plan, <u>backed by all</u>

(b) This Plan must look wider to attract, promote and/or improve, such as:-
   (i) Overseas visitors (especially Europeans) and Foreign students.
   (ii) Visiting Cruise Liners (e.g. Cowes, Sandown Bay).
   (iii) "Business Hospitality" jaunts from the Mainland.
   (iv) All-out drive and greater provision for the "Conference Trade".
   (v) All-year round "special" events (Musical, Pop, "Theme Weeks", Sports, Cultural, Rallies etc.) and Arena(s) for them as needed.
   (vi) Upgrading of many sea front areas - islandwide.
   (vii) Sheltered Yacht Marina facilities on S.E. coast.
   (viii) More and better "Wet Weather" facilities.
   (ix) Tourist car parking, in general.

Some of the Problems - Are the Islanders ready to accept "Tourism" as the main plank in the I.W. economy? What of the effects if, like Skye, the I.W. is eventually linked either by tunnel or bridge to the mainland? Clearly, a reduction in travel costs would be of great benefit BUT- as the writer sees matters, unless very carefully handled such gain would be lost by the total invasion of mainland coaches bringing their thousands on a "once round", all day, "I.W. Safari Tour" in which razzamataz will prevail. This prospect should horrify residents and environmentalists enough to ask if this is what they really want?

In the meantime, we can but survey the present steady loss of more hotels, increased demands for "B&B" accommodation, and chalet/tented/touring camping style holidays, already very popular, reflecting the growing change in style and habits of the current socio-economic groupings now holidaying in the I.W.

Short break holidays will increase, lower age groups will arrive seeking more excitement than rest and the erstwhile traditional fortnight family holiday in the Garden Isle will slowly reduce in importance unless vigorously pursued.

All in all - the author sees a paramount need to look again at the recommendations in (d) on page 50 in conjunction with (b) above. In this regard, the suggested Shanklin sea-front "Millenium" development is a commendable start.

As a complete alternative could the I. W. become so environmentally mature that it was able to sell itself as the "Island of Green Tourism"? The basis for which could be its many and obvious beauties, wildlife, landscape, history, geology, archaeology etc. or even because of its "Naturist Beaches" - surely an untapped market!

Finally, should it set up an Environmental Studies Centre as part of the University of the Wight suggested earlier, in the hope that it would attract students, worldwide, and thereby create the image it was seeking to promote. What a glorious vista but regrettably NO to most of these innovative ideas which simply could not produce enough revenue.

COMMUNICATIONS - What changes are likely to have taken place by 2,100?

(a) **Rail** - probably an early link through to Ventnor and, later to Newport and Cowes - perhaps monorail/vectrail?

- it may well be that eventually a link bridge or tunnel will have finally been forced through which could then be matched up with an ALL ISLAND L.R.T/M.R.T system that would displace the railway and ease the problems of road traffic - but would the huge investment capital needed ever be achieved; many would hope not! In my case, it seems unlikely before 2,100 A.D.

(b) **Roads** - the motor car will continue to dominate and ever larger freight vehicles will inexorably wear out the major roads.

- probable completion of a number of relief (by pass) schemes e.g. Brading, Sandown/Shanklin, Shalfleet etc.

- rethink on road highway networks, perhaps more "one way" routes introduced, with lower speed limits - even, perhaps, more car parks.

- more "traffic calming" in towns and villages.

(c) **Cycle tracks & parks** - here, there is enormous potential for Islandwide development and the next 100 years will see it evolve.

(d) **Bridges/Tunnels** -

(i) Trans Medina - most probable within next 50 years

(ii) Trans Solent - will continue to generate much argument but unless supported by a huge E . C. grant is unlikely to materialise in the next century, although . . . eventually!

(e) **Sea - Ferries, Ports, Creeks and Harbours**

A new ferry terminal could provide the opportunity for the I.W. Council to enter into the Trans Solent market, given adequate subsidy to do so. Fares will continue to increase until the Islanders take control of at least one major ferry crossing. Ideally this should be a comfortable Super Passenger Vessel service. Bembridge Harbour is likely to become moribund unless considerable dredging is undertaken to remove the silting that will happen faster than any rising sea levels or scouring. Shanklin Marina - a possibility?

(e) **Air** - although private flying and gliding will prosper, the most that can be foreseen in commercial aviation development in the next century is by helicopter. Charter flights could, however, well be introduced into a progressive tourist development both at home and abroad, both by fixed winged aircraft as well as by the larger helicopter similar to that in service to the Scilly Isles.

DEMOGRAPHY

Whether the population levels will rise or fall depends on so many different factors - the Island's economy, migration, housing, health, employment prospects and the age/sex structure. Taking all these things and the Author's opening remarks into account - who can tell?

On balance, the probability seems to indicate a continuing "natural decrease" in population, coupled with little change in the in-migration until the next census. After which, assuming the economy has by then improved, there seems every promise of the I.W. showing up to 4% rise each decade to around 150,000 before the year 2050. The peaceful quality of life on the Island will ensure that the older age groups continue to predominate, by comparison with the U. K. in general - but note the possible effect of this, under.

EMPLOYMENT

The more optimistic possibilities mentioned in the earlier part on "Industry" could each promote a much larger job market which, with an improving economy and/or E.C/Govt. grant would auger well for the I.W.

There is also the premise that the steady rise in the in-migration of elderly persons will in itself affect the balance and nature of employment in the I.W. This could apply in two ways:-

(a) Greater need for more social, welfare, hospital, health and support services in general (e.g. Care establishments, Day nurseries etc.)

(b) Meanwhile the reducing birth rates and growing out-migration of the economically active (16-60 years) would mean less demand on educational services (unless the I.W. achieves its own University?) and more productive employment opportunities being lost to the mainland.

All of which is pure conjecture but included to demonstrate the vagaries of prediction. What is certain though is the steady fall-off in full-time work, in favour of more part-time employment; seasonal work problems will increase dependent on the extension of all-year tourism; job mobility becomes a necessity and - a feature of life which is so true of the indigenous Islander - I.W. girls will continue to return to the Island from across the water with their husbands and partners.

SETTLEMENT

The correlation between population change and settlement change hinges on, both, employment and the housing market. When mainland prices are high and I.W. prices are lower - people tend to move.

In the coming years, it is suggested that;-

- Newport will increase in size and importance as Ryde reduces (see Commerce page 116).

- most other central townships will be kept fully alive in the high season only, and, then - mainly by the needs of tourism.

119

- there will be a continuing tendency for the I.W. population to move from north to south and from urban to rural areas with a natural preference for the coast.

INFRASTRUCTURE

More provision for "Healthy Living" facilities (e.g. The Heights at Sandown) will be needed as 'fitness' enthusiasm grows.

On the Renewable Energy front the coming century is likely to witness considerable advances; all new domestic building work may soon include solar heating panels, a trial off-shore Wind Farm and, possibly, simple Barrage or Wave Power experimental schemes are not beyond realisation.

ENVIRONMENTAL ISSUES

Waste - it is to be hoped that by the end of the next century burying waste in holes in the ground, as a matter of political expediency, will have become a thing of the past. In its wake Waste Resource Management Schemes will be in place to deal with its maximum use for energy production, recycling, composting and reclamation. In this, all commercial establishments will be expected to provide their own systems: several I.W. Companies already lead the way with their splendid environmental policies.

Land Drainage - Wetlands are worth protecting. We need to learn to store water on and in the land and, thus, to conserve more of our wetlands and wildlife. It is no bad thing to appreciate that flood plains are just that.

Pollution - dirty water discharge and sewage pollution of inshore waters will continue unless the utmost pressure is kept up. Hopefully, techniques will soon be available to turn <u>all</u> the sludge from the treatment works into a commercially acceptable fertiliser: all other polluted waste should be incinerated.

Apart from the above, there is a growing awareness of noise, smell and visual pollution that must continue to be closely monitored if the "quality of life criteria" are to be improved over the next century.

FINALLY The EARTH is a whole system and the ISLE OF WIGHT is only one very small part of it but it enjoys special features that make it unique and which must be protected for the benefit of its future generations.

As a final "Geographer's Look", we in the Island can peer into the next century, supported by the I.W. Unitary Development Plan that backs up the tenets of "Going for Green" to ensure just that. Yes, indeed, because of our environmental awareness - our real stock in trade - the I.W. in the year 2100 promises to remain a truly beauteous place to visit or, better, in which to live.